Sounds Great

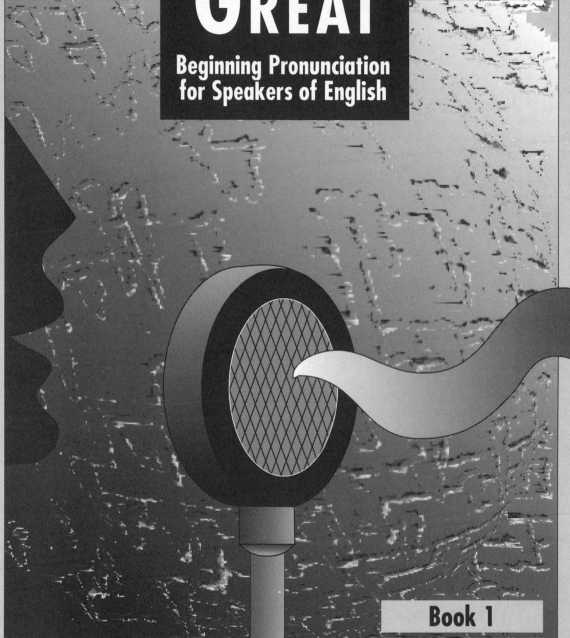

Beginning Pronunciation for Speakers of English

Book 1

Beverly Beisbier

Australia Canada Mexico Singapore Spain United Kingdom United States

The publication of *Sounds Great, Book 1:Beginning Pronunciation for Speakers of English,* was directed by the members of the Newbury House publishing Team at Heinle:

David C. Lee, Editorial Director
Gabrielle B. McDonald, Production Editor
Nancy Mann, Developmental Editor

Also participating in the publication of this program were:

Publisher: Stanley J. Galek
Editorial Production Manager: Elizabeth Holthaus
Managing Developmental Editor: Beth Kramer
Project Manager: Anita L. Raducanu/A+ Publishing Services
Assistant Editor: Kenneth Mattsson
Associate Marketing Manager: Donna Hamilton
Production Assistant: Maryellen Eschmann
Manufacturing Coordinator: Mary Beth Lynch
Illustrator: David Murray
Illustration Director: Len Shalansky
Interior Design: Robert Freese
Cover Illustrator and Designer: Bortman Design Group

Manufactured in the United States of America

Library of Congress Cataloging in Publication Data

Beisbier, Beverly.
Sounds great / Beverly Beisbier.
p. cm.
ISBN 0-8384-3964-0
1. English language--Pronunciation for foreign speakers.
2. English language--Textbooks for foreign speakers. I. Title.
PE1157.B45 1994
428.3'4--dc20 93-41029
CIP

ISBN: 0-8384-3964-0

20 19 18 17 16 15 14 13

Contents

To the Teacher

Sounds Great is a two-level series of American English pronunciation practice materials designed for learners of English as a second or foreign language. Book One is designed for learners at the high beginning level. Book Two is geared toward intermediate-level students.

The *Sounds Great* program presents and has students practice high-frequency pronunciation points that are both central to intelligibility and challenging for most learners of English regardless of native language. The emphasis of this program is not to teach complex rules, nor is the entire range of English stress, intonation, vowel, and consonant patterns included. Rather, the two books briefly present selected pronunciation points with student rule-writing and then provide extensive hands-on practice so that students can carry key pronunciation patterns over to interaction and communication with others. The many guided conversations, pair and small group practices, information gap activities, peer interviews, and short oral reports will invite students to enjoy improving their command of spoken English.

SPECIAL FEATURES OF *SOUNDS GREAT, BOOK ONE*

- Awareness-building drills and ear training exercises for word stress, sentence stress, intonation, and troublesome consonants and vowels
- Activities for recognition and discovery of pronunciation and spelling rules with student-generated rule writing
- Contextualized pronunciation practice exercises graded from controlled and semi-controlled to interactive and communicative
- Student-centered pair and small group activities
- Emphasis on word stress, sentence stress, and intonation as foundations for intelligible speech
- Structures and vocabulary accessible to learners at the high beginning level
- A wide variety of topics and activity types to stimulate student interest in and enjoyment of pronunciation and speaking

ORGANIZATION OF *SOUNDS GREAT, BOOK ONE*

The first eight lessons form the core of *Sounds Great, Book One*. These lessons teach students to recognize, practice, and use word stress, sentence stress, and intonation patterns. Lessons 9–14, which can be used selectively by the teacher, deal with high-frequency consonants, *-s* and *-ed* endings, and high-frequency vowels.

Each lesson starts with awareness-building drills and exercises, continues to pronunciation rule-writing and controlled activities, and then moves to semi-controlled and communicative interactive practice. Consonant and vowel lessons include spelling/sound correspondence through student analysis and rule-writing.

THE COMPLETE SOUNDS GREAT PROGRAM

Designed to complement the student text and provide teachers and students alike with a comprehensive pronunciation program, *Sound Great* includes the following carefully-developed components:

AUDIO PROGRAM

The *Audio Program* presents all *Intensive Practice*, *Pronounce Words*, *Pronounce Phrases*, *Pronounce Sentences*, and *Listening Discrimination* ear-training drills.

In the student text, the cassette symbol (📼) shows the drills, listening exercises, and examples recorded in the *Audio Program*.

The complete Tapescript is found in the *Instructor's Manual*.

INSTRUCTOR'S MANUAL

The *Instructor's Manual* offers suggested procedures for practice activities, correction and follow-up techniques, and answer keys. Appendix A provides a list of reference materials to diagnose students' pronunciation difficulties and suggested readings in the teaching of pronunciation. Appendix B classifies *Sounds Great* practice activities by grammar point, and Appendix C classifies them by topic.

Also included is the complete Tapescript of the *Audio Program*.

Acknowledgments

I am indebted to the teaching staff at The American Language Program of the American Center in Paris, especially to Bill Yaffe and Rick Willet, for their having encouraged me to write the wobbly beginnings of this textbook series years ago. Deepest appreciation also goes to the following instructors who patiently piloted material and tried to make it work for all of us: Rick Willet of the American Center in Paris (France), Matthew Hunt of California State University at Fullerton, and Donald Weasenforth and John Wong of the American Language Institute, University of Southern California. Double thanks to Day Jones of the ALI, USC, for endlessly piloting material, constantly giving feedback, and generally cheering me on.

I would also like to acknowledge the reviewers who comments help polish Book One: Charlotte Al-Jamal of Florida International University, Kyra Carroll of University of Oregon, Linda Grant of Georgia Institute of Technology, Polly Hildebrecht of University of Miami, Lois Lanier of University of Maryland, Sybil Senters of Language Studies International, Scott Stevens of University of Delaware, and Neil Williams of New York University.

Thanks also to Nancy Mann of Heinle & Heinle for her editorial guidance.

I have saved my biggest thanks for last. Thank you to those who have inspired and shaped this book more than anyone else—my students.

To the Student

Guide to Symbols and Figures

This symbol [cassette symbol] means you can listen to the *Sounds Great, Book 1,* cassette tape.

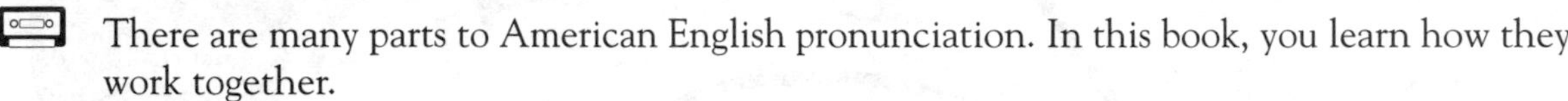

There are many parts to American English pronunciation. In this book, you learn how they work together.

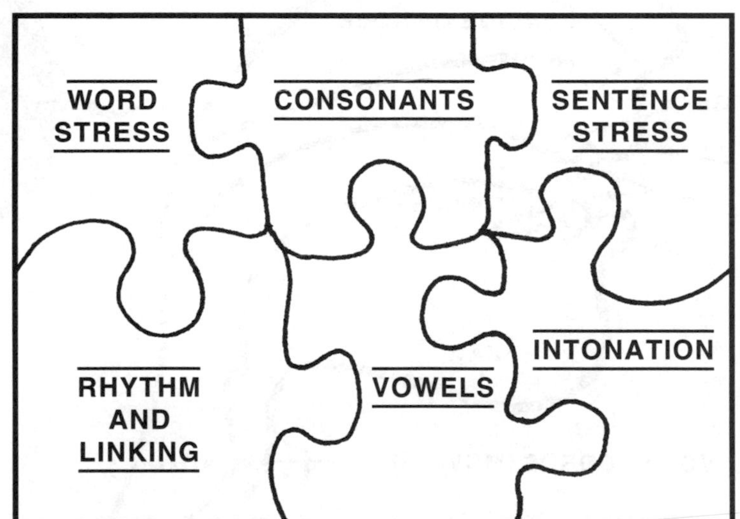

Circles and dots show word stress. Listen and repeat.

English hello animal tomorrow

Circles and dots show sentence stress, too. Listen and repeat.

I can pronounce English. We're writing you a letter.

Dots and arrows show intonation. Listen and repeat.

I want to hear a story. What's your name? Are you listening?

Here you see rhythm groups and linking.

It's a nice afternoon / for a picnic.

Here is a head. It's like your head.

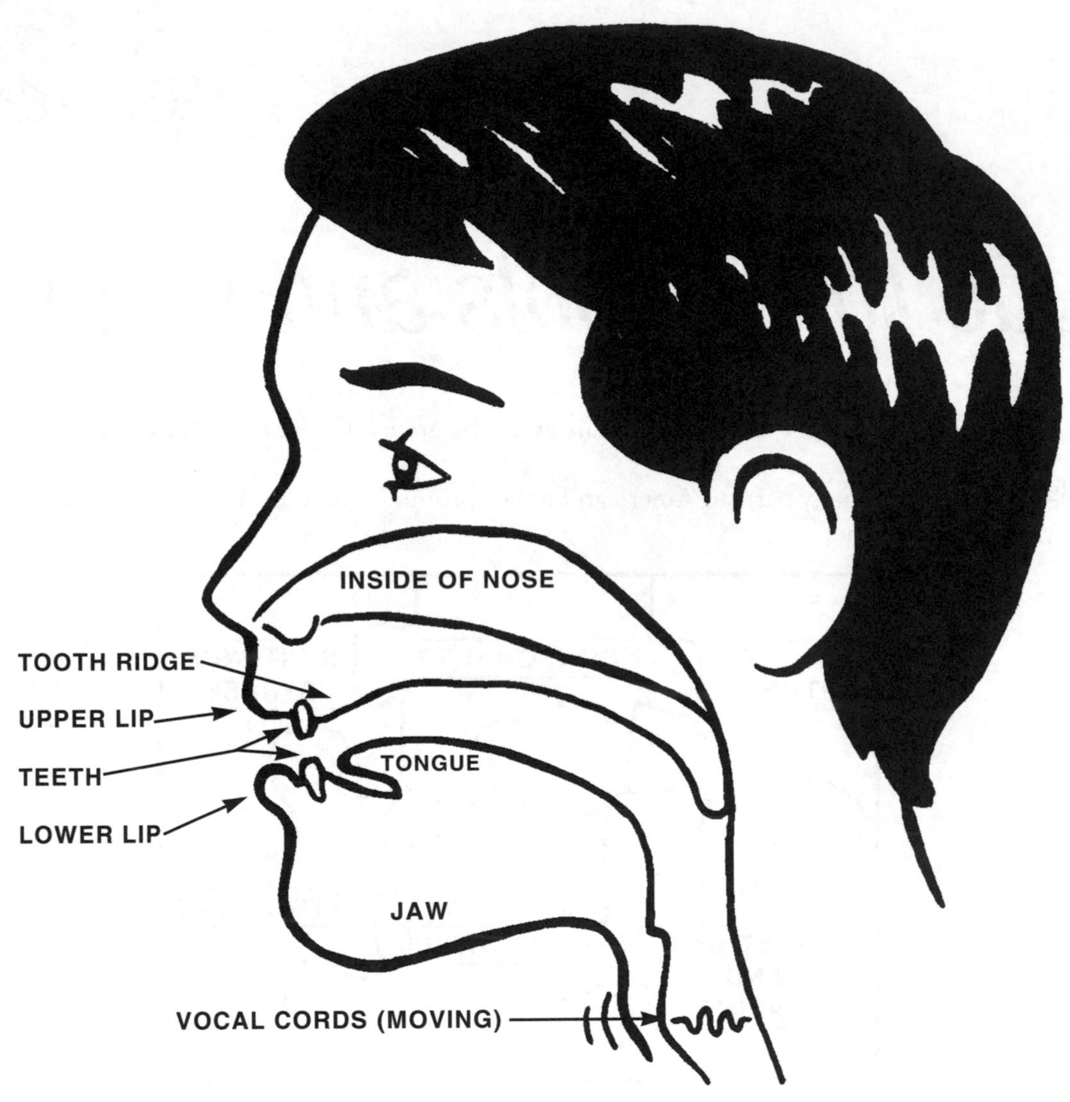

Here are some vowel sounds. Vowel sounds are sometimes different from letters. Vowel sounds are between lines like this: / /.

Vowel sound: /iy/ Vowel letters: eat

Listen to and repeat the vowel sounds and words.

1. /iy/ me, read
2. /ɪ/ is, it
3. /ɛ/ get, bread
4. /æ/ hat, after
5. /a/ lot, father
6. /ə/ up, mother
7. /ey/ eight, baby
8. /ow/ go, open
9. /ay/ my, night

These are lips.

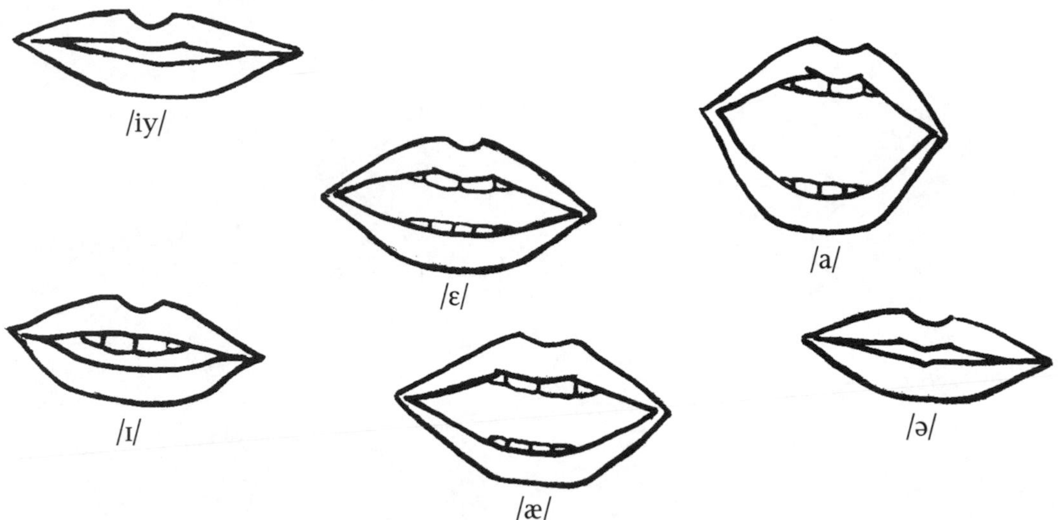

Here are some consonant sounds. Consonant sounds are sometimes different from letters, too. Consonant sounds are between lines like this: / /.

Consonant sound: /f/ Consonant letters: phone

 Listen to and repeat the consonant sounds and words.

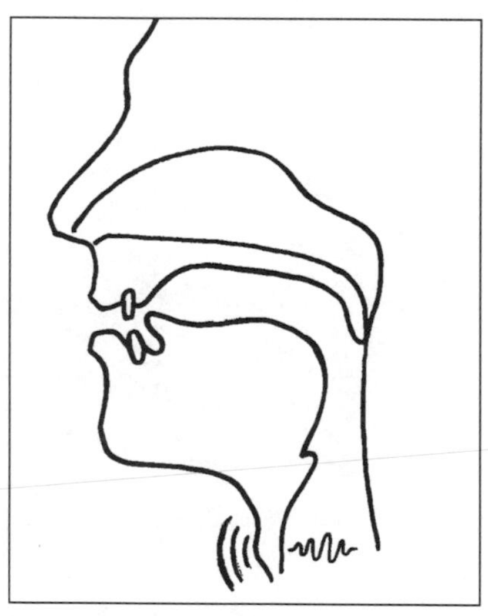

vocal cords moving

1. /b/ boy, about
2. /d/ day, need
3. /v/ very, live
4. /ð/ the, this
5. /z/ zoo, was
6. /dʒ/ just, age
7. /l/ look, believe
8. /r/ red, car
9. /y/ you, young

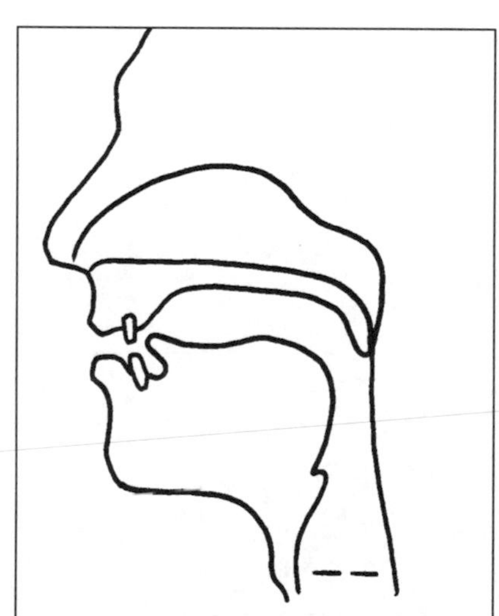

vocal cords not moving

10. /p/ pencil, drop
11. /t/ two, wait
12. /f/ find, before
13. /θ/ thin, with
14. /s/ see, city
15. /ʃ/ shop, wash
16. /tʃ/ child, match

LESSON 1

The Vowel /ə/

You need to pronounce /ə/ many times in words and sentences. You know this vowel. It is in words like *us, gum, up, the, was, does, one, come,* and *under.*

Contrasting the vowels /ə/ and /a/

Many students have some problems with /ə/ (as in *us*). /ə/ is different from the vowel /a/ (as in *hot*).

WARM-UP

Look at the pictures. Listen to the words and repeat them.

1. cut /ə/

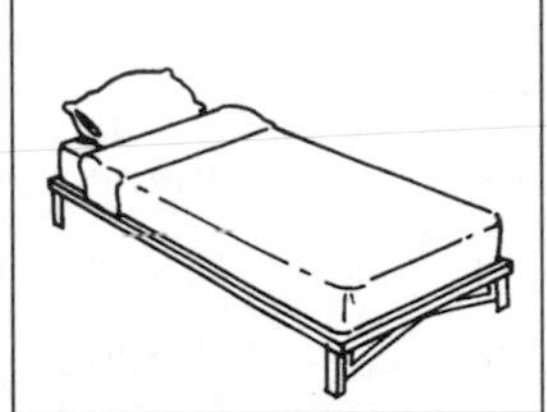

2. cot /a/

ARTICULATION

Look at the pictures. The heads and lips show how to make the sounds.

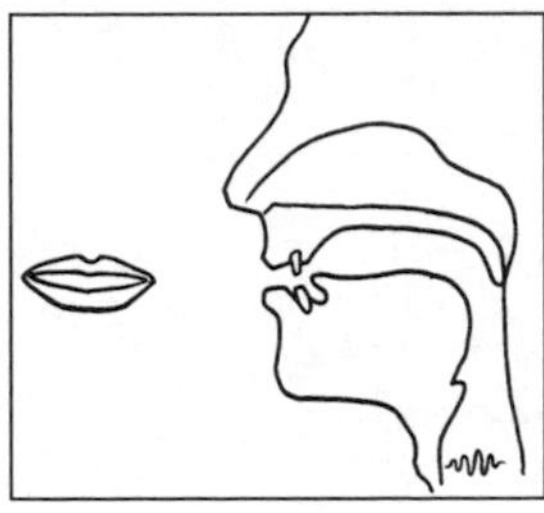

1. /ə/

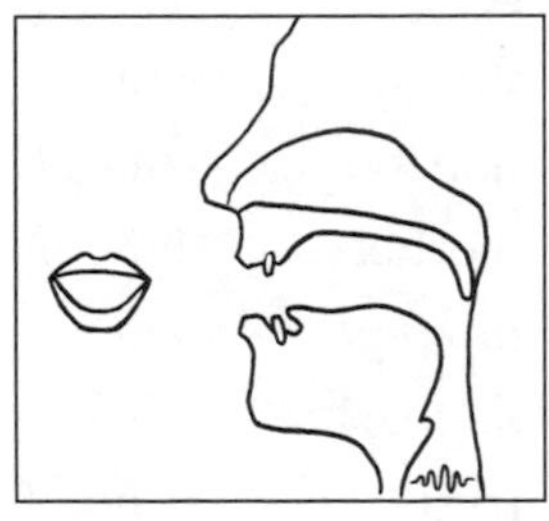

2. /a/

CONTRAST

Look at the pairs of words. Listen and repeat.

nut – not	luck – lock
run – Ron	cup – cop

LISTENING

Some words in English have the contrast between /ə/ and /a/ like the pairs of contrast words above. Look again at the *cut* and *cot* pictures on page 1. /ə/ is *number 1*. /a/ is *number 2*.

Listen to the following words. If you hear /ə/ as in *cut*, say "one." If you hear /a/ as in *cot*, say "two."

INTENSIVE PRACTICE

As a class, listen to and repeat the pairs of /ə/ and /a/ words you hear.

PRONOUNCE WORDS

Listen to and repeat the /ə/ words you hear.

PRONOUNCE PHRASES

Listen to and repeat the phrases you hear.

PRONOUNCE SENTENCES

Listen to and repeat the sentences you hear.

PRACTICE ACTIVITIES

1. LISTENING DISCRIMINATION. /ə/ and /a/.

DIRECTIONS: You are going to hear some pairs of words. Some words have /ə/. Some words have /a/. Circle *same* if the two words have the same vowel sound. Circle *different* if the two words have different vowel sounds.

EXAMPLES:

	bug	one	(same)	different
	rob	stuck	same	(different)
	not	bus	same	(different)
	follow	bother	(same)	different
1.	was	lot	same	different
2.	on	of	same	different
3.	come	got	same	different
4.	touch	the	same	different
5.	month	none	same	different
6.	father	mother	same	different
7.	drop	jump	same	different
8.	couple	double	same	different
9.	clock	trust	same	different
10.	money	funny	same	different

PARTNER 1

2a. LISTENING DISCRIMINATION AND SPEAKING. Pair Practice Words for /ə/ and /a/. PARTNER 1. Use this page. PARTNER 2. Turn to page 6.

DIRECTIONS: First you are the speaker. Say the words to your partner. You see the vowel sound before each word. For example, you say "Number 1 is *not*." Repeat any words your partner does not understand.

1. /a/ not
2. /ə/ cut
3. /ə/ done
4. /a/ sock
5. /ə/ color
6. /ə/ luck
7. /a/ Ron
8. /a/ shot
9. /ə/ bucks
10. /ə/ cup

Now you are the listener. Your partner will say some words. Circle the words you hear. Ask your partner to repeat any words you do not understand. Number 11 is an example.

11. (shut) shot
12. dull doll
13. cup cop
14. nut not
15. run Ron
16. color collar
17. cut cot
18. duck dock
19. luck lock
20. bucks box

Now compare answers with your partner.

PARTNER 1

3a. LISTENING DISCRIMINATION AND SPEAKING. Pair Practice Sentences for /ə/ and /a/. PARTNER 1. Use this page. PARTNER 2. Turn to page 6.

DIRECTIONS: First you are the speaker. Say the sentences to your partner. You see the vowel sound before each sentence. Repeat any sentences your partner does not understand.

1. /a/ I put the BOX away.
2. /ə/ There's a CUP in the kitchen.
3. /ə/ She SHUT it.
4. /ə/ He lost his LUCK.

Now you are the listener. Your partner will say some sentences. Circle the word you hear. Ask your partner to repeat any sentences you do not understand. Number 5 is an example.

5. I don't like this __________ .
   a. (color) b. collar
6. She said "__________ ."
   a. nut b. not
7. There's a __________ near the water.
   a. duck b. dock
8. I think it's __________ .
   a. done b. Don

Now compare answers with your partner.

4. SPEAKING. Pair or Group Practice for /ə/. Below you see a picture of boxes. Each box has an object in it.

DIRECTIONS: Take turns asking and answering questions about the boxes. Use the words *above* and *under*. You and your group need to pronounce /ə/ in your questions and answers.

EXAMPLE:

STUDENT 1: Where's the brush?
STUDENT 2: Above the nut. Where's the tongue?
STUDENT 3: Under the sun. Where's the rug?
STUDENT 1: Above the duck. Where's the . . .

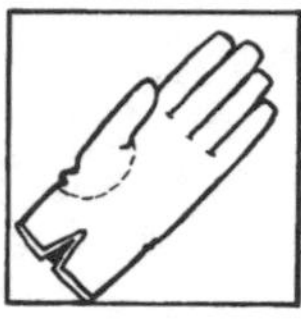
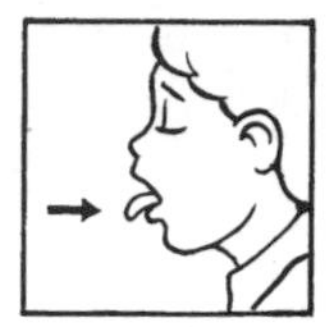

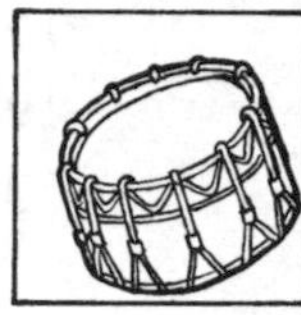

5. SPEAKING. Pair or Group Practice for /ə/. Below you see a family tree.

DIRECTIONS: Take turns asking and answering questions about the family tree. You and your group need to pronounce /ə/ in the family words and names.

EXAMPLE:

STUDENT 1: Who's Anita's husband?
STUDENT 2: Anita's husband is Douglas. Who's Thomas's brother?
STUDENT 3: Thomas's brother is Buster. Who's Gus's grandmother?
STUDENT 1: Gus's grandmother is Anita. Who's . . .

SYLLABLES AND SPELLING

You can find the vowel sound /ə/ in the spelling of words. Listen to the number of *syllables* in a word. A *syllable* is a beat in a word.

Listen to these words. Tap a pencil for the number of beats.

one syllable	*two syllables*	*three syllables*
go	listen	enjoying
he	baby	professor
can	other	seventeen
five	seven	beautiful
slow	answer	understand

Can you add some one-syllable words to the list? Can you add some two-syllable words? Do you know some three-syllable words?

FIGURE IT OUT

Many one-syllable words have the sound /ə/. You can look at the spelling of a word. Spelling helps you know when to pronounce a vowel like /ə/ in one-syllable words.

Here are some /ə/ words. Study the spelling of these words.

/ə/ fun nut bus up gum luck

How many vowel letters make the sound /ə/? What letter makes the sound /ə/? Write a spelling rule.

RULE

Say the sound /ə/ in a one-syllable word when the word is spelled with _____ vowel letter. The vowel letter is _____ .

Here are more words with the sound /ə/. Here are some words with the sound /a/, too. Study the spelling of these words.

/ə/		/a/	
ton	month	job	not
one	son	clock	lock
some	love	box	on

What letter makes the sound /ə/ and the sound /a/ in words with one syllable? Write the letter here: ______

Listen carefully to words spelled with this letter. You will learn some /ə/ and some /a/ words. You can look in your dictionary, too. Look up the word *dot*. Is the vowel sound /ə/ or /a/? Now look up the word *won*. Is the vowel sound /ə/ or /a/? Be sure you understand the pronunciation symbols in your dictionary.

There are exceptions to these rules. Here are some one-syllable /ə/ words with *two* vowel letters: *(ou) touch, rough, tough, young; (oe) does.*

Here are some one-syllable /ə/ words with one vowel letter. The vowel letter is not *u: was, what, the.*

PAIR PRACTICE: Partner 2

PARTNER 2

2b. LISTENING DISCRIMINATION AND SPEAKING. Pair Practice Words for /ə/ and /a/. PARTNER 2. Use this page. PARTNER 1. Turn to page 3.

DIRECTIONS: First you are the listener. Your partner will say some words. Circle the words you hear. Ask your partner to repeat any words you do not understand. Number 1 is an example.

1. nut (not)
2. cut cot
3. done Don
4. suck sock
5. color collar
6. luck lock
7. run Ron
8. shut shot
9. bucks box
10. cup cop

Now you are the speaker. Say the words to your partner. You see the vowel sound before each word. For example, you say "Number 11 is *shut*." Repeat any words your partner does not understand.

11. /ə/ shut
12. /ə/ dull
13. /a/ cop
14. /ə/ nut
15. /ə/ run
16. /a/ collar
17. /ə/ cut
18. /ə/ duck
19. /ə/ luck
20. /a/ box

Now compare answers with your partner.

PARTNER 2

3b. LISTENING DISCRIMINATION AND SPEAKING. Pair Practice Sentences for /ə/ and /a/. PARTNER 2. Use this page. PARTNER 1. Turn to page 3.

DIRECTIONS: First you are the listener. Your partner will say some sentences. Circle the word you hear. Ask your partner to repeat any sentences you do not understand. Number 1 is an example.

1. I put the ____________ away.
   a. bucks b. (box)
2. There's a ____________ in the kitchen.
   a. cup b. cop
3. She ____________ it.
   a. shut b. shot
4. He lost his ____________ .
   a. luck b. lock

Now you are the speaker. Say the sentences to your partner. You see the vowel sound before each sentence. Repeat any sentences your partner does not understand.

5. /ə/ I don't like this COLOR.
6. /a/ She said "NOT."
7. /ə/ There's a DUCK near the water.
8. /a/ I think it's DON.

Now compare answers with your partner.

LESSON 2

The Vowel /ɪ/

You often find the vowel /ɪ/ in the English language. You know this vowel in words like *is, in, it, with, live, little, big, six,* and *him.*

Contrasting the vowels /ɪ/ and /iy/

Many students have some problems with /ɪ/ (as in it). /ɪ/ is different from the vowel /iy/ (as in eat).

WARM-UP

Look at the pictures. Listen to the words and repeat them.

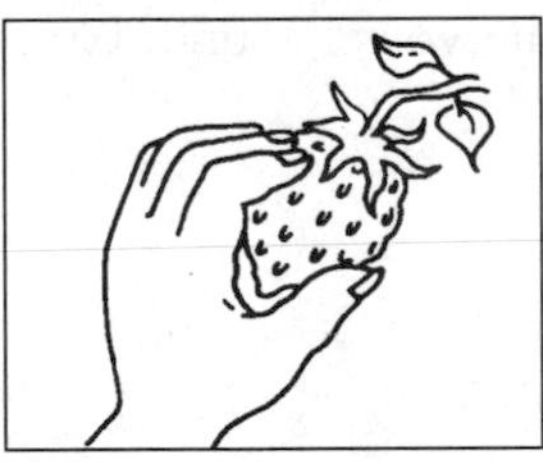

1. pick /ɪ/

2. peak /iy/

ARTICULATION

Look at the pictures. The heads and lips show how to make the sounds.

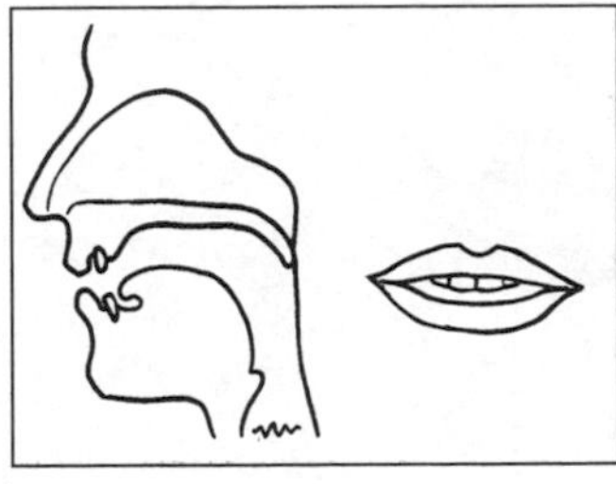

1. /ɪ/

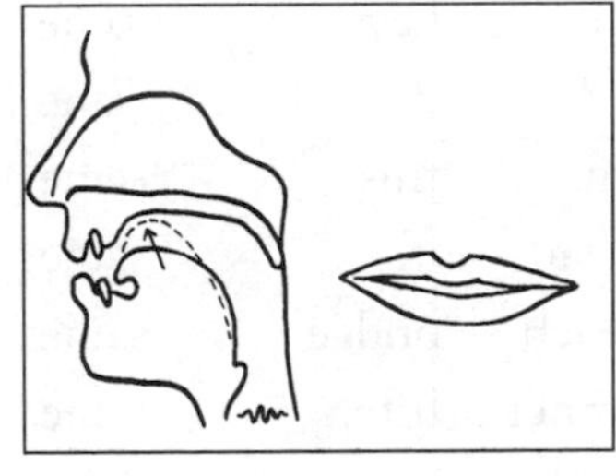

2. /iy/

CONTRAST

Look at the pairs of words. Listen and repeat.

his – he's	live – leave
it – eat	tin – teen

LISTENING

Many words in English have the contrast between /ɪ/ and /iy/. Look again at the *pick* and *peak* pictures on page 7. /ɪ/ is *number 1*. /iy/ is *number 2*.

Listen to the following words. If you hear /ɪ/ as in *pick*, say "one." If you hear /iy/ as in *peak*, say "two."

INTENSIVE PRACTICE

As a class, listen to and repeat the pairs of /ɪ/ and /iy/ words you hear.

PRONOUNCE WORDS

Listen to and repeat the /ɪ/ words you hear.

PRONOUNCE PHRASES

Listen to and repeat the phrases you hear.

PRONOUNCE SENTENCES

Listen to and repeat the sentences you hear.

PRACTICE ACTIVITIES

1. LISTENING DISCRIMINATION. /ɪ/ and /iy/.

DIRECTIONS: You are going to hear some pairs of words. Some words have /ɪ/. Some words have /iy/. Circle *same* if the two words have the same vowel sound. Circle *different* if the two words have different vowel sounds.

EXAMPLES:

	wind	kid	(same)	different
	fix	neat	same	(different)
	read	dish	same	(different)
	middle	sister	(same)	different
1.	miss	week	same	different
2.	sleeve	quick	same	different
3.	six	keys	same	different
4.	did	if	same	different
5.	trip	this	same	different
6.	mean	in	same	different
7.	peach	bridge	same	different
8.	dinner	listen	same	different
9.	thick	keep	same	different
10.	physics	business	same	different

PARTNER 1

2a. LISTENING DISCRIMINATION AND SPEAKING. Pair Practice Words for /ɪ/ and /iy/. PARTNER 1. Use this page. PARTNER 2. Turn to page 14.

DIRECTIONS: First you are the speaker. Say the words to your partner. You see the vowel sound before each word. For example, you say "Number 1 is *rich*." Repeat any words your partner does not understand.

1. /ɪ/ rich
2. /ɪ/ lip
3. /iy/ feet
4. /ɪ/ hill
5. /iy/ green
6. /iy/ lead
7. /iy/ cheap
8. /ɪ/ hit
9. /ɪ/ list
10. /ɪ/ bin

Now you are the listener. Your partner will say some words. Circle the words you hear. Ask your partner to repeat any words you do not understand. Number 11 is an example.

11. pitch (peach)
12. tin teen
13. sit seat
14. live leave
15. ship sheep
16. it eat
17. fill feel
18. his he's
19. bitten beaten
20. slip sleep

Now compare answers with your partner.

PARTNER 1

3a. LISTENING DISCRIMINATION AND SPEAKING. Pair Practice Sentences for /ɪ/ and /iy/. PARTNER 1. Use this page. PARTNER 2. Turn to page 14.

DIRECTIONS: First you are the speaker. Say the sentences to your partner. You see the vowel sound before each sentence. Repeat any sentences your partner does not understand.

1. /ɪ/ You can't put a SHIP in this room.
2. /iy/ We need a MEAL.
3. /iy/ Don't SLEEP on this rock.
4. /ɪ/ HIT this tool.

Now you are the listener. Your partner will say some sentences. Circle the word you hear. Ask your partner to repeat any sentences you do not understand. Number 5 is an example.

5. They can ____________ downtown.
   a. live b. (leave)
6. ____________ this cup.
   a. Fill b. Feel
7. Watch out for that ____________ .
   a. pick b. peak
8. I don't want this orange ____________ .
   a. pill b. peel

Now compare answers with your partner.

4. SPEAKING. Pair or Group Practice for /ɪ/. Below you see a picture of a crazy house. These things are in or near the crazy house:

a sink, a diamond ring, dishes, a bottle of milk, a fish, a plane ticket, bricks, string, a window, a little ship, a kitten, a shopping list, a big pig, a little pig, a six, pictures, a guitar

DIRECTIONS: Take turns asking and answering questions about the crazy house.

EXAMPLE:

STUDENT 1: Where's the string?
STUDENT 2: It's in the living room. Where are the pictures?
STUDENT 3: They're in the bathroom. Where's the guitar?

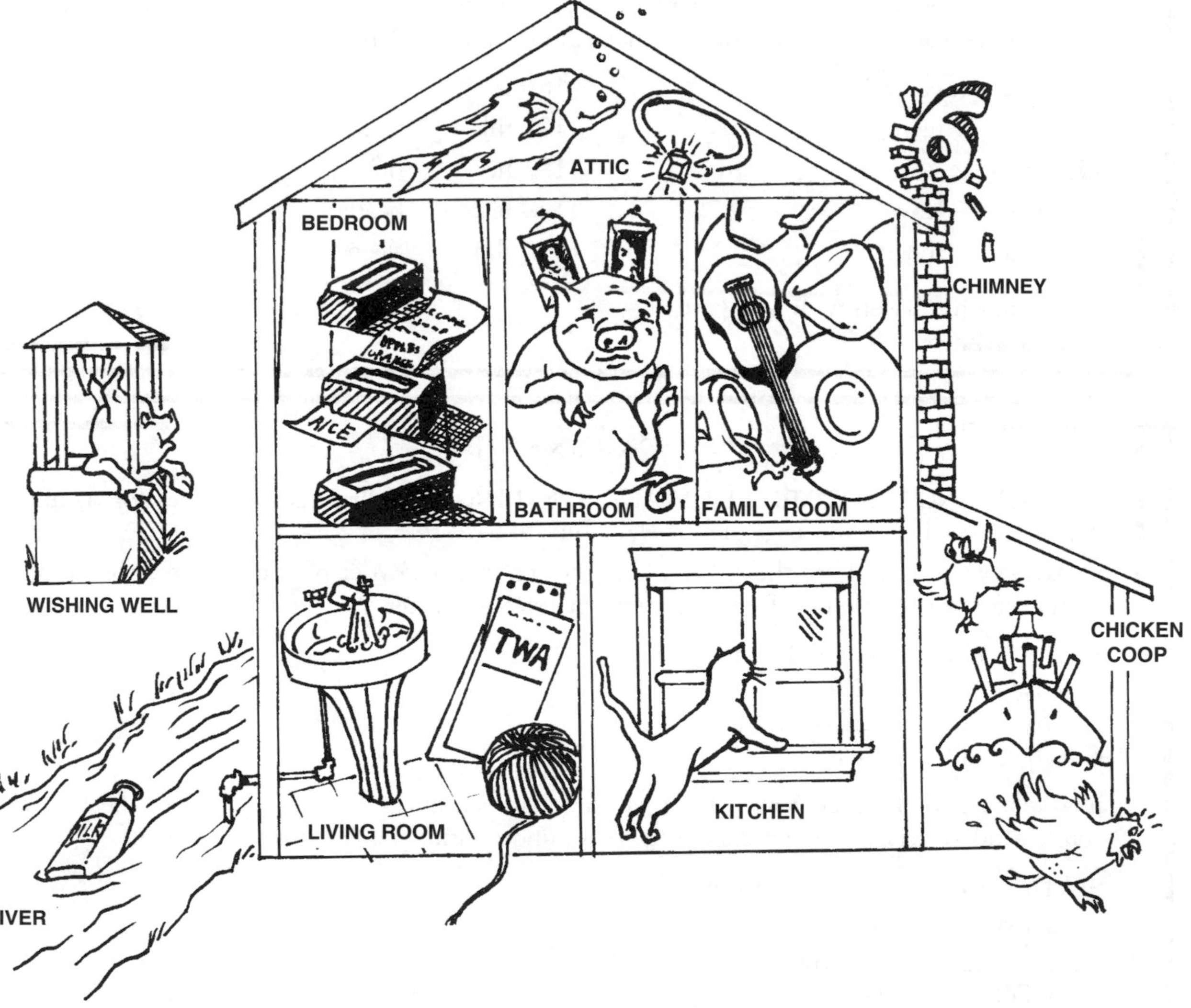

****Challenge!** Now ask questions again. Answer the questions with *two* prepositions.

EXAMPLE:

STUDENT 1: Where's the string?
STUDENT 2: It's in the living room next to the plane ticket. Where are the pictures?
STUDENT 3: They're in the bathroom near the big pig. Where's the guitar?

5. LISTENING DISCRIMINATION. Sit for It! Class Game to Practice /ɪ/.

DIRECTIONS: Stand up to start Round One of the game. You will hear four words. Three words have the /ɪ/ sound. One word does not have /ɪ/. Sit down when you hear the one word without /ɪ/.

Stand up again for Round Two. You will hear four new words. Again, sit down when you hear the one word without /ɪ/.

Pay attention! The word with no /ɪ/ can be the first word, the second word, the third word, or the last word. Your instructor will tell you to stand up for each new round. Your instructor or a student will keep score.

Who was able to sit at the sound of /ɪ/ most of the time? Who got better at the end of the game? Congratulations!

6. SPEAKING. Twenty Questions. Small Group Game to Practice /ɪ/.

DIRECTIONS: This is a guessing game. Work in groups of three or four. On a sheet of paper, write the name of each student in your group; this is your score sheet. Choose a role.

STUDENT 1: Think of an object in the classroom (like a book, a wastepaper basket, or a clock). Tell the name of the object to Student 2. Student 3 asks you about the object. Answer "No, it isn't" or "Yes, it is." You get one point if Student 3 does not guess the object after twenty questions.

STUDENT 2: Listen to the word that Student 1 tells you. Do not say the word aloud. Count Student 3's questions. If Student 3 guesses the correct object in fewer than twenty questions, give Student 3 one point on the score sheet. If Student 3 does not guess the object after twenty questions, stop the game. Give Student 1 one point on the score sheet.

STUDENT 3: Try to guess the object in the classroom that Student 1 is thinking of. Ask yes/no questions about the object. You get one point if you say the right object. You can ask only twenty questions.

STUDENT 4: Listen to Student 1 and Student 3. Be sure they pronounce the words *is* and *it* with the sound /I/. If they do not, make them repeat their questions or answers.

EXAMPLE:

STUDENT 3: Is it the clock?
STUDENT 1: No, it isn't.
STUDENT 3: Is it a book?
STUDENT 1: No, it isn't.
STUDENT 3: Is it the blackboard?
STUDENT 1: No, it isn't.

When a student has one point, all students choose a new role. Give the score sheet to the new Student 2. Your instructor will tell you when to stop playing the game.

Who has the most points in your group? Congratulations!

7. LISTENING DISCRIMINATION. Tick-Tack-Teak. Class Rhyme Game to Practice /ɪ/ and /iy/. A rhyme is a word that has the same vowel sound and ending sound as another word, for example, *live / give, meat / feet, boy /toy, mouse / house*. Except for the first sound, these rhyming words sound the same.

DIRECTIONS: Half of the class is Group X. Half of the class is Group O. Use Game Board A. Group X listens to the first word. Students in Group X find one word on the game board that rhymes with the first word. They put an X on the word with a pencil. Group O listens to the second word. Students in Group O find one word on the game board that rhymes with the second word. They put an O on the word with a pencil. The third word is for Group X, the fourth word is for Group O, the fifth word is for Group X, etc.

EXAMPLE:

GROUP X: You hear "kid." You put an X on "bid."
GROUP O: You hear "clean." You put an O on "mean."
GROUP X: You hear "trip." You put an X on "dip."
GROUP O: You hear "thin." You put an O on "win."

The winners of the game are the students who hear the /ɪ/ and /iy/ contrast. They will have three Xs or three Os in a row down, across, or diagonally. Say "Tick-Tack-Teak" when you have three marks in a row.

GAME BOARD A

READ	MEAN	HIT
TEACH	KEEP	WIN
DIP	EAT	BID

You can play another game of Tick-Tack-Teak with Game Board B.

GAME BOARD B

FISH	MEAL	QUEEN
WEEK	SKIN	WITCH
HILL	SICK	BEACH

8. SPEAKING. **Challenge! Supermarket "Chain." Class Memory Game to Practice /ɪ/ and /iy/.

DIRECTIONS: Your instructor will give you a list of food words with the vowel /ɪ/ and the vowel /iy/. Imagine that the whole class bought some food. Sit in a circle with your classmates. The first student says one food item. Then each student adds a new item and repeats all the food items of the other students.

EXAMPLE:

STUDENT 1: We bought tea.
STUDENT 2: We bought tea and chicken.
STUDENT 3: We bought tea, chicken, and bread sticks.
STUDENT 4: We bought tea, chicken, bread sticks, and peaches.

Who can accurately repeat the most food items in order? Congratulations!

SPELLING

FIGURE IT OUT

Many one-syllable words have the sounds /ɪ/ or /iy/. You can look at the spelling of a word. Spelling helps you know when to pronounce a vowel like /ɪ/ and when to pronounce it like /iy/.

Here are some /ɪ/ words and some /iy/ words. Study the spelling of these words.

/ɪ/	/iy/
fish	green
did	keep
pin	eat
with	speak
him	here
sing	these
if	cheese
big	piece

How many vowel letters make the sound /ɪ/? How many make the sound /iy/? What letter makes the sound /ɪ/? What letters make the sound /iy/? Write a spelling rule for each sound.

RULES

1. Say the sound /ɪ/ in a one-syllable word when the word is spelled with _____ vowel letter. The vowel letter is ________ .

2. Say the sound /iy/ in a one-syllable word when the word is spelled with _____ or _____ vowel letters. One vowel letter is always ______. The other vowel letters can be _____ , _____ , or _____ .

There are exceptions to these rules. Here are some one-syllable /ɪ/ words with two vowel letters: *give, live, build, been.*

Here are some one-syllable /iy/ words with only one vowel letter: *me, he, we, be.*

PARTNER 2

2b. LISTENING DISCRIMINATION AND SPEAKING. Pair Practice Words for /ɪ/ and /iy/. PARTNER 2. Use this page. PARTNER 1. Turn to page 9.

DIRECTIONS: First you are the listener. Your partner will say some words. Circle the words you hear. Ask your partner to repeat any words you do not understand. Number 1 is an example.

1.	(rich)	reach	6.	lid	lead
2.	lip	leap	7.	chip	cheap
3.	fit	feet	8.	hit	heat
4.	hill	heel	9.	list	least
5.	grin	green	10.	bin	bean

Now you are the speaker. Say the words to your partner. You see the vowel sound before each word. For example, you say "Number 11 is *peach*." Repeat any words your partner does not understand.

11.	/iy/	peach	16.	/iy/	eat
12.	/ɪ/	tin	17.	/ɪ/	fill
13.	/ɪ/	sit	18.	/iy/	he's
14.	/ɪ/	live	19.	/iy/	beaten
15.	/iy/	sheep	20.	/ɪ/	slip

Now compare answers with your partner.

PARTNER 2

3b. LISTENING DISCRIMINATION AND SPEAKING. Pair Practice Sentences for /ɪ/ and /iy/. PARTNER 2. Use this page. PARTNER 1. Turn to page 9.

DIRECTIONS: First you are the listener. Your partner will say some sentences. Circle the word you hear. Ask your partner to repeat any sentences you do not understand. Number 1 is an example.

1. You can't put a ___________ in this room.
   a. (ship) b. sheep
2. We need a ____________ .
   a. mill b. meal
3. Don't ___________ on this rock.
   a. slip b. sleep
4. ___________ this tool.
   a. Hit b. Heat

Now you are the speaker. Say the sentences to your partner. You see the vowel sound before each sentence. Repeat any sentences your partner does not understand.

5. /iy/ They can LEAVE downtown.
6. /iy/ FEEL this cup.
7. /ɪ/ Watch out for that PICK.
8. /ɪ/ I don't want this orange PILL.

Now compare answers with your partner.

LESSON 3

Word Stress: Two-Syllable Patterns

PART ONE Syllables

A **syllable** is a beat in a word. You can tap a pencil for each syllable in a word. Some words have only *one* syllable.

Listen to these words. Tap a pencil once for each word.
go, see, us, your, train, plate, on, down, five, one, night, week

This lesson is about words with *two* syllables.

Listen to these words. Tap a pencil twice for each word.
asking, listen, pencil, July, under, over, seven, sixteen, season, April

How many syllables are in your first name? What about your last name? Listen to your classmates. How many syllables are in their names?

PRACTICE ACTIVITY

LISTENING DISCRIMINATION.

DIRECTIONS: Listen to the words. How many syllables do you hear? Circle 1 if you hear only one syllable. Circle 2 if you hear two syllables.

EXAMPLES:

under	1	(2)
write	(1)	2

1.	dresses	1	2	7.	city	1	2
2.	fight	1	2	8.	watch	1	2
3.	twelve	1	2	9.	needed	1	2
4.	student	1	2	10.	paper	1	2
5.	many	1	2	11.	don't	1	2
6.	laugh	1	2	12.	very	1	2

PART TWO Syllables and Stress

Stress means that a syllable has a high tone. **Stress** means that a syllable is long and loud, too. English words with two syllables have *one* high, long, loud syllable. They have *one* low, short, quiet syllable.

Listen to the word. per son per son per son

The first syllable, *per,* has stress. *Per* is high, long, and loud. The second syllable, *son,* does not have stress. *Son* is low, short, and quiet. Most two-syllable English words are like the word *person*. The first syllable is high, long, and loud. The second syllable is low, short, and quiet.

Listen to and repeat these examples.

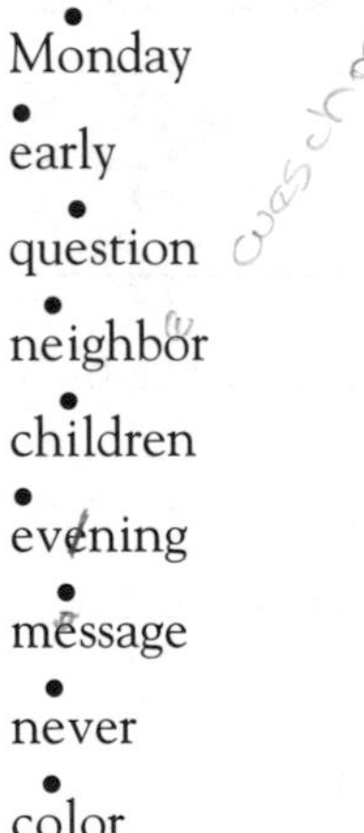

Monday
early
question
neighbor
children
evening
message
never
color

Listen to the word. to day to day to day

The first syllable, *to,* does not have stress. *To* is low, short, and quiet. The second syllable, *day,* has stress. *Day* is high, long, and loud. Some two-syllable English words are like the word *today*. The first syllable is low, short, and quiet. The second syllable is high, long, and loud.

Listen to and repeat these examples.

about
machine
alone
July
repeat
pronounce
himself
agree
surprise

PRACTICE ACTIVITIES

1. LISTENING DISCRIMINATION.

DIRECTIONS: Listen to the words. Mark the stressed syllable. Blacken the dot.

EXAMPLES:

Monday   about

1.	visit	5.	between	9.	without
2.	mistake	6.	story	10.	fifty
3.	after	7.	before	11.	people
4.	forget	8.	brother	12.	because

2. READ ALOUD.

DIRECTIONS: Now read the words above. Say the stressed syllable high, long, and loud.

3. LISTENING DISCRIMINATION.

DIRECTIONS: You will hear some words. Each word has two syllables. If you hear stress on the first syllable, say "first." If you hear stress on the second syllable, say "second."

EXAMPLES:

You hear *pencil*. You say: "First."

You hear *before*. You say: "Second."

4. LISTENING DISCRIMINATION.

DIRECTIONS: You will hear two words. Circle *same* if the two words have the same stressed syllable. Circle *different* if the two words do not have the same stressed syllable.

EXAMPLES:

	number	color	(same)	different
	because	pretty	same	(different)
	only	receive	same	(different)
1.	table	ago	same	different
2.	oranges	apple	same	different
3.	lesson	yellow	same	different
4.	polite	person	same	different
5.	maybe	letter	same	different
6.	believe	hotel	same	different
7.	office	begin	same	different
8.	quiet	busy	same	different
9.	forget	doctor	same	different
10.	music	repair	same	different

PART THREE /ə/ and /ɪ/ In Syllables Without Stress

A syllable that is low, short, and quiet does not have stress. Most low, short, quiet syllables in English have the vowel sound /ə/ or /ɪ/.

Listen to the syllables without stress in these words; they sound like /ə/ as in *us*.

promise around minute arrive table question business taken

Listen to the syllables without stress in these words; they sound like /ɪ/ as in *it*.

visit between city receive money classes office decide invite

There are many different ways to spell a low, short, quiet syllable. Spelling differences do not change the pronunciation of /ə/ or /ɪ/ in syllables without stress.

PRACTICE ACTIVITIES

1. LISTENING DISCRIMINATION.

DIRECTIONS: Listen to the following sentences. Some words have two syllables. Underline the words with two syllables.

EXAMPLE:

Two students were absent.

1. The room is quiet.
2. My pencil is broken.
3. I'll see you on Friday.
4. The office is closed now.
5. Her husband is a doctor.
6. She was very polite.
7. Your answer is correct.
8. You can leave a message later.
9. Michael is a very famous writer.
10. She studies English at a private school.

Now listen to the sentences again. Put a black dot over the stressed syllable in each word you underlined.

EXAMPLE:

Two students were absent.

2. READ ALOUD.

DIRECTIONS: Read the sentences above. Say the stressed syllables high, long, and loud. Pronounce syllables without stress like /ə/ or /ɪ/.

PARTNER 1

3a. LISTENING DISCRIMINATION AND SPEAKING. Pair Practice for Two-Syllable Words.
PARTNER 1. Use this page. PARTNER 2. Turn to page 25.

DIRECTIONS: First you are the speaker. Say the two words to your partner. Pronounce the stressed syllables high, long, and loud. Pronounce the syllable without stress like /ə/ or /ɪ/. Some pairs of words have the same stress pattern. Some pairs of words have a different stress pattern. Your partner will circle *same* or *different*. Repeat any words your partner does not understand.

EXAMPLES:

into	under	(same)	different
woman	tonight	same	(different)

1. people water
2. away needed
3. begin hello
4. along study
5. mistake hurry

Now you are the listener. Your partner will say some words. Circle *same* if the two words have the same stress pattern. Circle *different* if the two words have a different stress pattern. Ask your partner to repeat any words you do not understand.

6.	police	kitchen	same	different
7.	express	become	same	different
8.	glasses	angry	same	different
9.	career	practice	same	different
10.	spoken	instead	same	different

Now compare answers with your partner.

PART FOUR Stress Change In Numbers

Listen to the words. Blacken the dot over the stressed syllable.

1. fifty fifteen
2. thirty thirteen
3. fourteen forty
4. seventy seventeen
5. sixteen sixty
6. eighty eighteen

FIGURE IT OUT

Numbers with *-ty*
Which syllable is stressed, first or second? How do you pronounce the letter *t*, like /t/ or like /d/? Listen to the words again. Write a rule.

RULE

Numbers with *-ty* have stress on the _______________ syllable. The *t* sounds like /   /.

Numbers with *-teen*.
Which syllable is stressed, first or second? How do you pronounce the letter *t*, like /t/ or like /d/? Listen to the words again. Write a rule.

RULE

Numbers with *-teen* have stress on the _______________ syllable. The *t* sounds like /   /.

PRACTICE ACTIVITIES

PARTNER 1

1a. LISTENING DISCRIMINATION AND SPEAKING. Pair Practice. PARTNER 1. Use this page. PARTNER 2. Turn to page 26.

DIRECTIONS: First ask some questions. Then circle the answer you hear. Ask your partner to repeat any answers you do not understand. Number 1 is an example.

1. How many people were at your party? about 14 (about 40)
2. How old is Janet? 18 80
3. How much does this shirt cost? 15 dollars 50 dollars
4. How many stamps do you need? 17 70
5. How old is your friend? 16 60
6. What gate can I find my plane at? Gate 19 Gate 90
7. Which player dropped the ball? Number 18 Number 80
8. How many questions did she miss on the test? 13 30

Now listen to your partner's questions. Then say the answers. Stress the correct syllable in numbers. Pronounce *t* like /t/ for *-teen* words. Pronounce *t* like /d/ for *-ty* words. Repeat any answers your partner does not understand.

9. Fifteen times.
10. Ninety dollars.
11. I have seventy.
12. He's sixteen.
13. There are forty.
14. Number eighty, I think.
15. Thirteen names.
16. Sixteen.

Now compare answers with your partner.

 **2. LISTENING DISCRIMINATION. Tick-Tack-Number. Class Game to Practice Numbers.**

DIRECTIONS: Use Game Board A. You will hear some numbers. Put an X on the number you hear. Use a pencil. Say "Tick-Tack-Number" when you have four Xs in a row down, across, or diagonally.

GAME BOARD A

14	70	15	60
20	11	40	19
30	13	80	18
90	17	16	50

You can play another game of Tick-Tack-Number with Game Board B.

GAME BOARD B

113	118	140	117
170	114	110	190
119	150	180	116
111	160	115	130

3. READ AND REPORT. Group or Class Activity to Practice Numbers.

DIRECTIONS: Flyers are pieces of paper. You sometimes find them in your mailbox. Flyers tell you about food and other things you can buy. Your instructor will give you a flyer or ask you to bring a flyer to class. Tell other students about your flyer. Talk about prices, stores, dates, and other things you read on your flyer.

EXAMPLES:

"Pete's Grocery has a sale this week. The sale ends May 15. Oranges are 50 cents a pound. What a bargain!"

"Big Boy Electronics has a sale this month. The sale ends May 31. VCRs are $150. What a bargain!"

PART FIVE Compound Nouns

Classroom and *notebook* are compound nouns. You can see two parts in a compound noun: *class + room* and *note + book*. There are many compound nouns in English. Sometimes we write the two parts as one word, like *classroom*. Sometimes we write the two parts as two words, like *bus driver*.

FIGURE IT OUT

All two-syllable compound nouns have the same stress pattern.

Listen to the words. Blacken the dot over the stressed syllable.

1. suitcase
2. football
3. earring
4. girlfriend
5. restroom
6. airplane
7. workbook
8. headache

Which part of a compound noun has stress, the first part or the second part? Write a rule for stress in compound nouns.

RULE

In two-syllable compound nouns, the __________ part has stress.

PRACTICE ACTIVITIES

1. READ ALOUD.

DIRECTIONS: Here are some compound nouns you probably know. Read them. Stress the first part of each word.

1. passport
2. bedroom
3. baseball
4. hairbrush
5. weekend
6. drugstore
7. classmate
8. teaspoon
9. bookstore

PARTNER 1

2a. LISTENING DISCRIMINATION AND SPEAKING. Who Does It? Pair Practice.

PARTNER 1. Use this page. PARTNER 2. Turn to page 26.

DIRECTIONS: First ask some questions. Then listen to your partner's answers. Correct your partner if the first part is not stressed. Repeat any questions your partner does not understand.

1. Who drives a cab?
2. Who paints signs?
3. Who counts money at a bank?
4. Who examines people's eyes?
5. Who puts out fires?
6. Who makes dresses?
7. Who washes dishes?
8. Who delivers milk?

Now listen to your partner's questions. Use one of the professions from the list to answer. Stress the first part. Ask your partner to repeat any questions you do not understand.

PROFESSIONS

A bus driver
A car dealer
A disk jockey
A doorman
A French teacher
A mailman
A news reporter
A truck driver

3. SPEAKING. Guided Conversation to Practice Compound Nouns.

DIRECTIONS: Here is a shopping list and a list of stores. Take turns asking and answering questions about the things on the list. Stress the first part of compound nouns.

EXAMPLE:

SHOPPER: Do you know where I can buy a hairbrush?
FRIEND: At the drugstore.
SHOPPER: Thanks.
FRIEND: You're welcome.

SHOPPING LIST

some toothpaste
a notebook
a baseball
some sport socks
some cough drops
a bookmark
some shoe polish
some bath soap
a backpack
a skateboard
a candy bar
a hairbrush

STORES

bookstore
candy store
drugstore
shoe store
toy store

MODEL CONVERSATION

SHOPPER: Do you know where I can buy ____________________ ?
FRIEND: At the ____________________ .
SHOPPER: Thanks.
FRIEND: You're welcome.

4. SPEAKING. **Challenge! Room-*er*. Class Memory Game to Practice Compound Nouns.

DIRECTIONS: Your instructor will give you a list of objects. Most are compound nouns and some are not. Sit in a circle with your classmates. Think of every kind of *room* you know in a house or building. The first student asks where to find an object on the list. The second student answers with the name of a room. Take turns asking and answering, going around the circle.

EXAMPLE:

STUDENT 1: Where can you find a night-light?
STUDENT 2: In a bedroom. Where can you find a notebook?
STUDENT 3: In a classroom. Where . . .

Your instructor will tell you if your answer is not logical. Then ask your classmate to repeat the name of the object. Answer with the name of a different room that you think is correct.

FIGURE IT OUT

You have learned that:

1. numbers ending in *-ty* have stress on the first syllable
2. numbers ending in *-teen* have stress on the second syllable
3. compound nouns have stress on the first part

What about other two-syllable words? How can you know which syllable to stress? Most two-syllable words have stress on the first syllable. Most of the time you need to stress the first syllable.

Look at these two-syllable words with stress on the first syllable.

pencil, paper, mother, carpet, table, sofa, question, building, science,
photo, letter, garden, language, money, engine, happy, angry, famous,
honest, busy, careful, pretty, handsome, perfect, quiet, heavy, ready, modern

What part of speech are they? Nouns? Verbs? Adjectives? Adverbs? Prepositions? Write a rule.

RULE

Most two-syllable ________________ and ___________________ have stress on the first syllable.

About 20 percent of two-syllable words have stress on the second syllable. Now look at these two-syllable words with stress on the second syllable.

decide, return, agree, become, arrive, escape, invite,
explain, receive, begin, prepare, relax, above,
behind, around, across, between, below, away

What part of speech are they? Nouns? Verbs? Adjectives? Adverbs? Prepositions? Write a rule.

RULE

Some two-syllable _______________ and ___________________ have stress on the second syllable.

There are many exceptions to these general rules. Can you think of a two-syllable verb with stress on the first syllable? Can you think of a two-syllable preposition with stress on the first syllable?

Summary: In general, stress the first syllable of a two-syllable word. If the word is a *verb* or a *preposition*, it may be stressed on the second syllable. Only a small number of *nouns* and *adjectives* have stress on the second syllable. You will learn more about how to recognize first or second syllable stress in Lesson 4.

Now you know that stress is important in words with more than one syllable. Listen to the vocabulary words you learn. Learn their stress patterns *and* their meaning.

PART SIX Stress In Dictionaries

Sometimes you learn vocabulary when you read. Then you do not hear stress. If you need to know stress, you can look in a dictionary.

Look up the word *expect* in your dictionary. Is it clear which syllable has stress? Look up the word *happen* in your dictionary. Is it clear which syllable has stress?

If you do not understand stress marks in your dictionary, ask your instructor.

PARTNER 2

3b. LISTENING DISCRIMINATION AND SPEAKING. Pair Practice for Two-Syllable Words. PARTNER 2. Use this page. PARTNER 1. Turn to page 19.

DIRECTIONS: First you are the listener. Your partner will say some words. Circle *same* if the two words have the same stress pattern. Circle *different* if the two words have a different stress pattern. Ask your partner to repeat any words you do not understand.

EXAMPLES:

into	under	(same)	different
woman	tonight	same	(different)

1.	people	water	same	different
2.	away	needed	same	different
3.	begin	hello	same	different
4.	along	study	same	different
5.	mistake	hurry	same	different

Now you are the speaker. Say the two words to your partner. Pronounce the stressed syllable high, long, and loud. Pronounce the syllable without stress like /ə/ or /ɪ/. Some pairs of words have a different stress pattern. Your partner will circle *same* or *different*. Repeat any words your partner does not understand.

6. police kitchen
7. express become
8. glasses angry
9. career practice
10. spoken instead

Now compare answers with your partner.

PAIR PRACTICE: Partner 2

PAIR PRACTICE: Partner 2

PARTNER 2

1b. LISTENING DISCRIMINATION AND SPEAKING. Pair Practice. PARTNER 2. Use this page. PARTNER 1. Turn to page 20.

DIRECTIONS: First listen to your partner's questions. Then say the answer. Stress the correct syllable in numbers. Pronounce *t* like /t/ for *-teen* words. Pronounce *t* like /d/ for *-ty* words. Repeat any answers your partner does not understand.

1. About forty.
2. She's eighty.
3. Fifteen dollars.
4. Seventeen.
5. He's sixteen.
6. Gate nineteen.
7. Number eighty.
8. Thirteen.

Now ask some questions. Then circle the answer you hear. Ask your partner to repeat any answers you do not understand. Number 1 is an example.

9. How many times did he call you? (15 times) 50 times
10. How much is this calculator? 19 dollars 90 dollars
11. How many books do you have? 17 70
12. How old is Tyler? 16 60
13. How many cards are there on the table? 14 40
14. Which horse will win the race? Number 18 Number 80
15. How many names are on the list? 13 30
16. How many ounces are in a pint? 16 60

Now compare answers with your partner.

PARTNER 2

2b. LISTENING DISCRIMINATION AND SPEAKING. Who Does It? Pair Practice. PARTNER 2. Use this page. PARTNER 1. Turn to page 22.

DIRECTIONS: First listen to your partner's questions. Use one of the professions from the list to answer. Stress the first part. Ask your partner to repeat any questions you do not understand.

PROFESSIONS

A bank teller
A cab driver
A dish washer
A dress maker
An eye doctor
A fireman
A milkman
A sign painter

Now ask some questions. Then listen to your partner's answers. Correct your partner if the first part is not stressed. Repeat any questions your partner does not understand.

9. Who teaches French?
10. Who sells cars?
11. Who reports the news?
12. Who drives a truck?
13. Who delivers mail?
14. Who plays records on the radio?
15. Who stands by a door?
16. Who drives a bus?

Word Stress: Predictable Three-Syllable Patterns

LESSON 4

In this lesson, you find out about stress in some three-syllable words. You also find out about endings, like *open* + *er* and *quiet* + *ly*. Endings help you find the correct word stress.

PART ONE Word Building with *-er, -or,* and *-ly*

Here are some examples of three-syllable nouns and adverbs. You can build nouns from verbs by adding *-er* or *-or*. You can build adverbs from adjectives by adding *-ly*.

PRACTICE ACTIVITIES

1. LISTENING DISCRIMINATION.

DIRECTIONS: Listen to the following two-syllable and three-syllable words. Mark the stressed syllable of the words. Blacken the dot.

EXAMPLE: collect collector

verb	*noun*	*adjective*	*adverb*
travel	traveler	nervous	nervously
visit	visitor	fluent	fluently
erase	eraser	correct	correctly
manage	manager	rapid	rapidly
instruct	instructor	complete	completely
listen	listener	perfect	perfectly

2. READ ALOUD.

DIRECTIONS: Now read the pairs of words in activity 1 above. Say the stressed syllable high, long, and loud.

FIGURE IT OUT

When you build words and add *-er*, *-or*, or *-ly*, does the loud syllable of the word change? Write a rule.

RULE

To build a word with *-er*, *-or*, or *-ly*, find out which syllable is stressed in a verb or adjective. Then add *-er*, *-or*, or *-ly*. The stressed syllable *(circle one)* changes does not change.

PARTNER 1

3a. LISTENING DISCRIMINATION AND SPEAKING. Pair Practice for Three-Syllable *-er* and *-or* words. PARTNER 1. Use this page. PARTNER 2. Turn to page 33.

DIRECTIONS: First ask some questions. Then listen to your partner's answers. Correct your partner if the right syllable is not stressed. Repeat any questions your partner does not understand.

1. Who manages?
2. Who visits a sick person?
3. Who is beginning to study English?
4. Who reports the news?
5. Who directs movies?
6. Who works in a garden?
7. Who gives advice?
8. Who collects things?

Now listen to your partner's questions. Use one of the professions from the list to answer. Stress the right syllable. Ask your partner to repeat any questions you do not understand.

PROFESSIONS

A follower	A lecturer	A programmer	A researcher
An inventor	A performer	A publisher	A translator

PARTNER 1

4a. LISTENING DISCRIMINATION AND SPEAKING. Pair Practice for Three-Syllable *-ly* Adverbs. PARTNER 1. Use this page. PARTNER 2. Turn to page 33.

DIRECTIONS: Say these sentences to your partner. Then your partner will say sentences with *-ly* words. Correct your partner if the right syllable is not stressed. Repeat any sentences your partner does not understand.

1. He's a reckless driver.
2. They're rapid learners.
3. He's a graceful dancer.
4. She's a quiet speaker.
5. They're polite listeners.
6. She's a careful worker.

Now listen to your partner's sentences. Respond using sentences with *-ly* words.

EXAMPLE:

YOUR PARTNER: They're clever thinkers.
YOU: You're right. They *think cleverly*.

Stress the right syllable of the *-ly* words. Ask your partner to repeat any sentences you do not understand.

PART TWO Three-Syllable Words Ending In *consonant + y*

PRACTICE ACTIVITIES

1. LISTENING DISCRIMINATION.

DIRECTIONS: These three-syllable words end in a consonant letter + the letter *y*. Listen to the words. Mark the stressed syllable. Blacken the dot.

EXAMPLE: company (● o o)

factory	history	currency	faculty
battery	energy	pharmacy	chemistry
grocery	agency	specialty	poetry

2. READ ALOUD.

DIRECTIONS: Now read the words in section **1** above. Say the stressed syllable high, long, and loud.

FIGURE IT OUT

Which syllable is stressed in three-syllable words ending in *consonant* + *-y*? Is it the first, second, or third syllable? Write a rule.

RULE

In three-syllable words ending in *consonant* + *-y*, stress the ________________ syllable.

PARTNER 1

3a. LISTENING DISCRIMINATION AND SPEAKING. Name It! Pair Practice for Stress in *consonant* + *-y* Words. PARTNER 1. Use this page. PARTNER 2. Turn to page 34.

DIRECTIONS: First ask some questions. Your partner will answer with a three-syllable *consonant* + *-y* word. Be sure your partner stresses the word correctly. Repeat any questions your partner does not understand.

1. What do you call a place to buy food?
2. What is another word for dollars and yen?
3. Where can you see works of art?
4. What do you call a place where workers make things?
5. Where can you find lots of books?
6. What is the word for 100 years?

Now your partner will ask you some questions. Choose a three-syllable word from the word bank to answer. Stress the word correctly. Ask your partner to repeat any questions you do not understand.

Name It! Word Bank

an agency a bakery a battery chemistry jewelry a pharmacy

4. SPEAKING. Pair or Group Practice for Stress in *consonant* + *-y* Words. Below you see a picture of Littletown. You can see different places.

DIRECTIONS: Take turns asking and answering questions about the places. Use prepositions from the list. You and your group need to stress the right syllable of *consonant* + *-y* words.

EXAMPLE:

STUDENT 1: Where's the bakery?
STUDENT 2: It's between the agency and the grocery. Where's the pharmacy?
STUDENT 3: It's near the jewelry shop. Where's the . . .

PREPOSITIONS
between near across from

LITTLETOWN

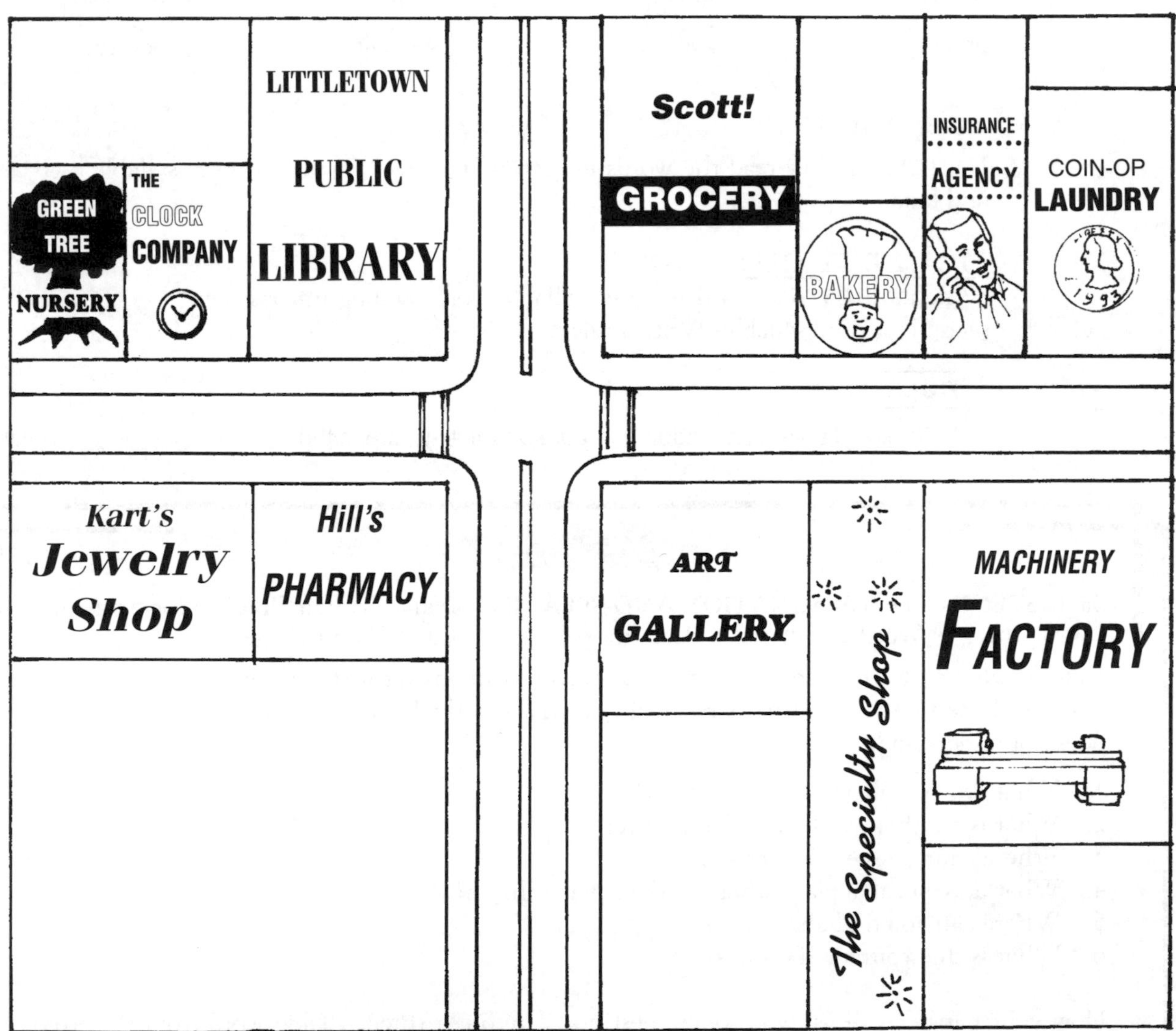

****Challenge!** Now ask questions again. Answer the questions with *two* prepositions.

EXAMPLE:

STUDENT 1: Where's the bakery?
STUDENT 2: It's near the laundry between the agency and the grocery. Where's the pharmacy?
STUDENT 3: It's near the jewelry shop across from the gallery. Where's the . . .

PART THREE Words Ending in *-ion*

Thousands of words in English end in *-ion*. Some of them have two or three syllables. You will learn how to find the stressed syllable in these words.

PRACTICE ACTIVITIES

1. LISTENING DISCRIMINATION.

DIRECTIONS: Listen to these words. Mark the stressed syllable. Blacken the dot.

EXAMPLES:

● ○ station   ○ ● ○ construction

○ ○ nation	○ ○ ○ attention
○ ○ action	○ ○ ○ profession
○ ○ question	○ ○ ○ opinion
○ ○ billion	○ ○ ○ vacation
○ ○ fashion	○ ○ ○ conclusion
○ ○ onion	○ ○ ○ location

2. READ ALOUD.

DIRECTIONS: Now read one word from each column across. Stress the high, long, loud syllable.

EXAMPLE:

● nation	● billion
● attention	● vacation

FIGURE IT OUT

Which syllable is stressed in words ending in *-ion*? Write a rule.

RULE

Words ending in *-ion* have the high, long, loud stress on the syllable

_________________ *-ion*.

PARTNER 1

3a. SPEAKING AND LISTENING. Pair Practice for Stress in *-ion* Words. PARTNER 1. Use this page. PARTNER 2. Turn to page34. Kim does many interesting things. Here you see Kim's calendar. It shows some things Kim did in May. Your partner has Kim's May calendar, too.

DIRECTIONS: For each day with *, Kim was busy. Ask questions about the days with *. Take turns asking and answering questions. You and your partner need to stress the syllable before *-ion*.

EXAMPLE:
STUDENT 1: What did Kim do May 20th?
STUDENT 2: She went to a lecture on tradition. What did Kim do May 2nd?
STUDENT 1: She went to an inspection of the new library. What did . . .

Kim's Appointments **MAY**

Sunday	Monday	Tuesday	Wednesday	Thursday	Friday	Saturday
	1	2 inspection of the new library	3 *	4	5 *	6 auction
7	8 *	9	10	11 convention	12 *	13
14 station to pick up a friend	15	16	17 movie about fashion	18 *	19	20 *
21	22	23 *	24 session on college tuition	25 *	26	27 discussion on famous writers
28	29 *	30 show on new inventions	31			

PARTNER 2

3b. LISTENING DISCRIMINATION AND SPEAKING. Pair Practice for Three-Syllable *-er* and *-or* words. PARTNER 2. Use this page. PARTNER 1. Turn to page 28.

DIRECTIONS: First listen to your partner's questions. Use one of the professions from the list to answer. Stress the right syllable. Ask your partner to repeat any questions you do not understand.

PROFESSIONS

An advisor
A beginner
A collector
A director
A gardener
A manager
A reporter
A visitor

Now ask some questions. Then listen to your partner's answers. Correct your partner if the right syllable is not stressed. Repeat any questions your partner does not understand.

9. Who invents machines?
10. Who gives lectures?
11. Who translates?
12. Who programs computers?
13. Who follows a leader?
14. Who performs on a stage?
15. Who does research?
16. Who publishes books?

PARTNER 2

4b. LISTENING DISCRIMINATION AND SPEAKING. Pair Practice for Three-Syllable *-ly* Adverbs. PARTNER 2. Use this page. PARTNER 1. Turn to page 28.

DIRECTIONS: Listen to your partner's sentences. Respond using sentences with *-ly* words.

EXAMPLE:

YOUR PARTNER: They're clever thinkers.
YOU: You're right. They *think cleverly*.

Stress the right syllable of the *-ly* words. Ask your partner to repeat any sentences you do not understand.

Now say these sentences to your partner. Then your partner will say sentences with *-ly* words. Correct your partner if the right syllable is not stressed. Repeat any sentences your partner does not understand.

7. They're honest players.
8. He's a nervous driver.
9. She's a fluent speaker.
10. He's a careless worker.
11. They're cautious swimmers.
12. He's a selfish player.

PARTNER 2

3b. LISTENING DISCRIMINATION AND SPEAKING. Name It! Pair Practice for Stress in *consonant + -y* Words. PARTNER 2. Use this page. PARTNER 1. Turn to page 29.

DIRECTIONS: First your partner will ask you some questions. Choose a three-syllable word from the word bank to answer. Stress the word correctly. Ask your partner to repeat any questions you do not understand.

Name It! Word Bank

a century   currency   a factory   a gallery   a grocery   a library

Now ask some questions. Your partner will answer with a three-syllable *consonant + -y* word. Be sure your partner stresses the word correctly. Repeat any questions your partner does not understand.

7. Where can you buy vitamins and drugs?
8. Where does an agent work?
9. What do you call the study of chemicals and elements?
10. What makes a car start?
11. Where can you buy cake and bread?
12. What do you call rings, bracelets, and necklaces?

PARTNER 2

3b. SPEAKING AND LISTENING. Pair Practice for Stress in *-ion* Words. PARTNER 2. Use this page. PARTNER 1. Turn to page 32. Kim does many interesting things. Here you see Kim's calendar. It shows some things Kim did in May. Your partner has Kim's May calendar, too.

DIRECTIONS: For each day with *, Kim was busy. Ask questions about the days with *. Take turns asking and answering questions. You and your partner need to stress the syllable before *-ion*.

EXAMPLE:
STUDENT 1: What did Kim do May 20th?
STUDENT 2: She went to a lecture on tradition. What did Kim do May 2nd?
STUDENT 1: She went to an inspection of the new library. What did . . .

Kim's Appointments **MAY**

Sunday	Monday	Tuesday	Wednesday	Thursday	Friday	Saturday
	1	2 *	3 election	4	5 collection of art	6 *
7	8 dinner with a companion	9	10	11 *	12 convention	13
14 *	15	16	17 *	18 Miami on vacation	19	20 lecture on tradition
21	22	23 session on college admission	24 *	25 find a location for a meeting	26	27 *
28	29 discussion on connections in business	30 *	31			

LESSON **5**

Sentence Stress, Unstress, and Rhythm

You learned that some syllables in words are stressed. Now you will learn that some words in sentences are stressed, too. Stressed words in a sentence are long and loud. Some stressed words are high, too.

Here are some words with stressed syllables and some sentences with stressed words. Compare them.

two syllables	*three syllables*
become	discover
I won.	You love her.
decide	divided
She cried.	We ride it.
polite	understand
You're right.	It's a man.
hello	afternoon
Let's go.	This is June.

PART ONE Stressed Words in Sentences

This lesson is about stressed words in sentences. You will learn which words in sentences are long and loud. You will learn which words are short and quiet.

PRACTICE ACTIVITIES

1. LISTENING DISCRIMINATION.

DIRECTIONS: Listen to the phrases. Mark the stressed word. Blacken the dot.

EXAMPLE: on the bus

1. in a class
2. on the phone
3. out of town
4. at a store
5. in the car
6. out the door
7. at a gym
8. on a date

FIGURE IT OUT

Which words are stressed in the phrases? Which words are *not* stressed in the phrases? Write some rules.

RULE FOR NOUNS

Nouns are *(circle one)* stressed not stressed.

RULE FOR ARTICLES AND PREPOSITIONS

Articles and prepositions are *(circle one)* stressed not stressed.

2. READ ALOUD.

DIRECTIONS: Now read the phrases above. Say the stressed words high, long, and loud.

3. LISTENING DISCRIMINATION.

DIRECTIONS: Listen to the short sentences. Mark the stressed word. Blacken the dot.

EXAMPLE: I know him.

1. We work.
2. It fell.
3. He met us.
4. You need it.
5. They see you.
6. You like her.
7. He lost it.
8. We hear him.

FIGURE IT OUT

Which words are stressed in the short sentences? Which words are *not* stressed in the sentences? Write some rules.

RULE FOR VERBS

Verbs are *(circle one)* stressed not stressed.

RULE FOR PRONOUNS

Pronouns are *(circle one)* stressed not stressed.

4. READ ALOUD.

DIRECTIONS: Now read the sentences above. Say the stressed words high, long, and loud.

5. READ ALOUD.

DIRECTIONS: Here are some sentences. Use your rules for stressed and unstressed words. Put a dot over the *stressed* words in the sentences.

EXAMPLES:

He stopped at a store.

We came to the class.

1. He works in a lab.
2. They played at the park.
3. She read some books.
4. You took a test.
5. I came in the room.
6. They made their beds.
7. She likes cats.
8. He lives in a house.
9. They eat after work.
10. She sent him a card.
11. I left the keys on the bus.
12. She shopped for a dress for the dance.

Now read your sentences aloud. Say the stressed words high, long, and loud.

PARTNER 1

6a. LISTENING DISCRIMINATION AND SPEAKING. Where Is It? Pair Practice.

PARTNER 1. Use this page. PARTNER 2. Turn to page 50.

DIRECTIONS: First ask some questions. Your partner will answer with a short phrase. Repeat any questions your partner does not understand.

1. Where did you park your bicycle?
2. Where did you put your suitcase?
3. Where did you play baseball?
4. Where did you wait for a bus?
5. Where did you put your money?
6. Where did you buy your shirt?
7. Where did you find the phone?

Now listen to your partner's questions. Use one of the phrases from the list to answer. Stress the noun in the phrase. Ask your partner to repeat any questions you do not understand.

PHRASES

in my room
on a chair
in class
on the desk
at the gym
at a shop
in the lab

PART TWO More Sressed Words In Sentences

You know you need to stress nouns and verbs in sentences. You know that prepositions, articles, and pronouns are not stressed. Here are some more examples. You will learn more about which words are stressed and unstressed.

PRACTICE ACTIVITIES

1. LISTENING DISCRIMINATION.

DIRECTIONS: Listen to the sentences. Mark the stressed words. Blacken the dots.

EXAMPLE:

She is tired.

1. It was a good day.
2. They are young men.
3. I have good news.
4. He has smart friends.
5. The gray car is old.
6. She can wear her new dress.
7. I have some fresh fruit.
8. We were best friends.

FIGURE IT OUT

Each sentence above has the verb *to be*, the verb *to have*, or a helping (auxiliary) verb. Some sentences have adjectives. Write some rules for the verb *to be*, the verb *to have*, helping verbs, and adjectives.

RULE FOR THE VERB *TO BE,* THE VERB *TO HAVE,* AND HELPING VERBS

The verb *to be,* the verb *to have,* and helping verbs are *(circle one)*
stressed not stressed.

RULE FOR ADJECTIVES

Adjectives are *(circle one)* stressed not stressed.

2. READ ALOUD.

DIRECTIONS: Now read the sentences above. Say the stressed words high, long, and loud.

3. LISTENING DISCRIMINATION.

DIRECTIONS: Listen to the sentences. Mark the stressed words. Blacken the dots.

EXAMPLE:

That man can run fast.

1. Give him those gloves and shoes.
2. This book is short but good.
3. He bought these suits and ties.
4. Joe and Sue like that car.
5. This is the day and year.
6. She knows him well.
7. He works hard.
8. I can read and type fast.
9. They sang the song well.
10. We drove the car fast.

Home work

FIGURE IT OUT

There are some new kinds of words in these sentences, too. Some sentences have *this, that, these,* and *those* and the words *and* and *but*. Some sentences have adverbs. Write a rule for demonstrative pronouns *(this, that, these, those)* and adverbs. Write another rule for conjunctions *(and, but)*.

RULE FOR DEMONSTRATIVE PRONOUNS AND ADVERBS

Demonstrative pronouns and adverbs are *(circle one)* stressed not stressed.

RULE FOR CONJUNCTIONS

Conjunctions are *(circle one)* stressed not stressed.

4. READ ALOUD.

DIRECTIONS: Now read the sentences at the bottom of page 38. Say the stressed words high, long, and loud.

FIGURE IT OUT

Here is a chart. Use *all* your rules for stressed and unstressed words. Complete the chart. You see an example.

Summary of Stressed and Unstressed Words in Sentences			
Stressed Words	**Example**	**Unstressed Words**	**Example**
nouns	*bird, pencil*		

5. READ ALOUD.

DIRECTIONS: Here are some sentences. Use your chart in "Figure It Out" on page 39 to find the stressed words. Put a dot over the *stressed* words in the sentences.

EXAMPLES:

The train came to town late.

She left a black purse at the bank.

1. This watch can show you the date and the time.
2. He washed and dried his face and hands.
3. Ted can read French fast and well.
4. I need a cup of milk and a spoon of salt.
5. The month of March has a lot of days.
6. She lost her key to the house.
7. They come to class late but work hard.
8. It was a dark night, and the rain fell hard.

Now read your sentences aloud. Say the stressed words high, long, and loud.

6. LISTENING DISCRIMINATION. Stressed Words with More Than One Syllable.

DIRECTIONS: Here are some sentences. Some words in the sentences have *two* or *three* syllables. Listen to the sentences. Mark the stressed syllables or words. Blacken the dots.

EXAMPLE:

The concert started at seven.

1. Candy answered slowly and carefully.
2. These machines can staple your papers.
3. He often listens to music in the car.
4. The children were happy to get new bicycles.
5. They can take a vacation in July and August.
6. A heavy notebook was on the lowest shelf.
7. It happened at the party at midnight.
8. The doctors were helping many sick patients.

Some stressed words have two or three syllables. Where do you need to put stress when these words are in sentences?

7. READ ALOUD.

DIRECTIONS: Now read the sentences above. Say the stressed syllables or words high, long, and loud.

8. SPEAKING. Guided Conversation to Practice Sentence Stress.

DIRECTIONS: Here is a list of new things you just bought. Here is a list of stores, too. Use the model conversation. Take turns as the Friend and the Shopper. Stress your sentences correctly.

EXAMPLE:

FRIEND: I like your new *belt*.

SHOPPER: Oh, thank you. I got it at the *dress shop*.

FRIEND: I like your new *shoes*.

SHOPPER: Oh, thank you. I got them at the *shoe store*.

NEW THINGS		STORES
jacket	racket	shoe store
shoes	socks	dress shop
tie	belt	bookstore
skis	dictionary	men's shop
boots	coat	sports shop
dress	sweatshirt	

MODEL CONVERSATION

FRIEND: I like your new ______________ .

SHOPPER: Oh, thank you. I got it/them at the ______________ .

PARTNER 1

9a. LISTENING DISCRIMINATION AND SPEAKING. Pair Practice Sentence Completion.

PARTNER 1. Use this page. PARTNER 2. Turn to page 51.

DIRECTIONS: First say some phrases to your partner. Stress the phrases correctly. Your partner needs to create a complete sentence from each phrase. Repeat any phrases your partner does not understand.

EXAMPLE:

YOU: at the bank

YOUR PARTNER: I saw my instructor at the bank.

Or: The teller at the bank was polite.

Or: I opened an account at the bank.

1. on Monday
2. at the library
3. by the telephone
4. in the kitchen
5. on a bus
6. to the instructor
7. in the morning

Now listen to your partner's phrases. Use the phrases to create a sentence. You can use the phrase in any part of your sentence.

EXAMPLE:

YOUR PARTNER: by the sofa

YOU: The table by the sofa has a drawer.

Or: He can find my notebook by the sofa.

Or: Let's put these lamps by the sofa.

Stress the correct syllables and words in your sentences.

PART THREE Unstressed /ə/ and /ɪ/ and Rhythm

You learned that most unstressed syllables in English words have the sound /ə/ or /ɪ/. Most unstressed syllables and words in sentences have the vowel sound /ə/ or /ɪ/, too.

Listen to the syllables and words without stress in these sentences; they sound like /ə/ or /ɪ/.

> The woman in line was angry.
> He listened and asked some questions.
> A train will arrive in a minute.
> A lot of people can sit at this table.
> A pen or a pencil is all that you need.

You hear stressed syllables and words. You hear unstressed syllables and words between them. Stressed and unstressed syllables and words in sentences make a pattern. This regular pattern is called **rhythm.**

Now listen to and repeat the sentences. Tap a finger or pencil for each stressed syllable or word. Say the unstressed syllables low, short, and quiet.

PRACTICE ACTIVITIES

PARTNER 1

1a. SPEAKING AND LISTENING. Pair Practice for Stress, Unstress, and Rhythm.
PARTNER 1. Use this page. PARTNER 2. Turn to page 51.

DIRECTIONS: Tom is having a party. You have a list of things Tom needs. Your partner has a list, too. You want to know all the things on Tom's list. Take turns asking and answering questions to complete your list. Stress the nouns and verbs in your answers. Do not stress the articles and prepositions.

EXAMPLE:

YOU:	Does Tom still need Coke?
YOUR PARTNER:	Yes, he needs twelve cans of Coke. Does Tom still need potato chips?
YOU:	Yes, he needs a bag of potato chips. Does . . .

TOM'S PARTY LIST

____________ bread	____________ candy
a pound of cheese	____________ pickles
____________ popcorn	____________ peanuts
a package of pretzels	a carton of juice
12 cans of Coke	____________ milk
a bag of potato chips	a package of napkins
a box of cookies	a package of balloons

2. SPEAKING. What Is It? Class Game to Practice Sentence Stress, Unstress, and Rhythm.

DIRECTIONS: Sit in a circle with your classmates. Your instructor will tell a student to start the game. Study the example below. The first student makes a sentence with *it* and one or two phrases. The second student answers. Then the second student says a sentence with *it* and a phrase. The third student answers. Continue the game, going around the room.

EXAMPLE:
STUDENT 1: It's on the wall by the door. What is it?
STUDENT 2: A poster. It's on the floor by the window. What is it?
STUDENT 3: A bookcase. It's . . .

3. READ ALOUD.

DIRECTIONS: Here are some expressions. Do you remember which words are stressed and unstressed? Put dots over the stressed syllables and words. You can use your "Summary of Stressed and Unstressed Words in Sentences" on page 39 if you do not remember.

1. fat as a pig
2. dry as a bone
3. strong as an ox
4. red as a beet
5. light as a feather
6. blind as a bat
7. busy as a bee
8. white as a sheet
9. quiet as a mouse
10. flat as a pancake

Now read the expressions aloud.

4. SPEAKING.

DIRECTIONS: Look at the two examples below. After each expression, you see a sentence.

EXAMPLES:

strong as an ox ⟶ The boxer was strong as an ox.
white as a sheet ⟶ The child is afraid, and she's white as a sheet.

Now you do it. Make complete sentences with the expressions in section 3 above. Use your own ideas. Say the stressed and unstressed syllables and words correctly.

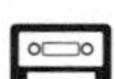

5. LISTENING DISCRIMINATION.

DIRECTIONS: Here are some proverbs. Listen to them. Put dots over the stressed syllables and words.

EXAMPLE: Variety is the spice of life.

1. The early bird catches the worm.
2. Two is company, but three is a crowd.
3. When the cat's away, the mice play.
4. Honesty is the best policy.
5. Seeing is believing.
6. Money burns a hole in the pocket.
7. Practice makes perfect.
8. Look before you leap.
9. The best things in life are free.
10. A little knowledge is a dangerous thing.

Now read the proverbs aloud.

6. REPORT.

DIRECTIONS: Choose one proverb from section **5** on page 43. You can use your dictionary if you do not know all the words in the proverb. Tell the class the meaning of the proverb. Give an example of the proverb.

EXAMPLE:
My proverb is "Variety is the spice of life." *Variety* means different things. *Spice* is something you put in food. Spice makes food taste good. The proverb means different things in life make life good. A person with many different jobs believes that "variety is the spice of life."

PART FOUR Stress In Negative Sentences

You learned about stressed and unstressed syllables and words in sentences. You know unstressed syllables and words often have /ə/ or /ɪ/ sounds. Stress and unstress make rhythm in English sentences.

Here you will learn more about stressed words in sentences. Now the sentences are negative.

PRACTICE ACTIVITIES

1. LISTENING DISCRIMINATION.

DIRECTIONS: Listen to the negative sentences. Mark the stressed syllables and words. Blacken the dots.

EXAMPLE: He isn't at home.

1. I'm not working.
2. We don't need paper.
3. This isn't my wallet.
4. They can't remember.
5. We weren't ready.
6. She didn't call me.
7. They aren't in class.
8. There's not enough time.

FIGURE IT OUT

Which new words are stressed in the negative sentences? Write a rule.

RULE FOR NEGATIVE WORDS

Negative words *(not, don't, can't)* are *(circle one)* stressed not stressed.

Now turn to page 39. Put this information on your chart "Summary Of Stressed and Unstressed Words in Sentences."

2. READ ALOUD.

DIRECTIONS: Now read the negative sentences above. Say the stressed words high, long, and loud.

3. SPEAKING. Pair or Group Practice Pictures for Negative Sentence Stress.

DIRECTIONS: Below you see some pictures of people doing different things. Take turns asking and answering questions about the people. Make questions that need *no* for an answer. Stress your questions and answers correctly.

EXAMPLE:

STUDENT 1: Is Joe riding a bike?
STUDENT 2: No, Joe isn't riding a bike. Are Kay and Tony swimming?
STUDENT 3: No, Kay and Tony aren't swimming. Is . . .

4. READ ALOUD. *Can* and *Can't*. Helping verbs are not stressed. *Can* is a helping verb. Sentences with *can* do not have stress on *can*. The vowel in *can* sounds like /ə/ as in the word <u>u</u>s. Negative words are stressed. Negative sentences with *can't* have stress on *can't*. The vowel in *can't* sounds like /æ/ as in the word c<u>a</u>t.

DIRECTIONS: Listen to and repeat the pairs of sentences with *can* and *can't*.

EXAMPLES:

I can read fast. He can't read fast.
/ə/ /æ/

Bob can speak German. Joe can't speak German.
/ə/ /æ/

They can answer your question. We can't answer your question.
/ə/ /æ/

The vowels and rhythm in *can* and *can't* sentences are different. Each sentence with *can't* has one more stress.

Now you try it. Read the following sentences aloud. Stress the word *can't*. Do not stress *can*. Say the vowel in *can* like /ə/.

1. Joe can type fast.
2. Bob can't read French.
3. I can't come to class.
4. I can come to the party.
5. The doctor can help you.
6. The nurse can't help you.
7. I can't remember his number.
8. I can remember his name.

PARTNER 1

5a. LISTENING DISCRIMINATION AND SPEAKING. Pair Practice Sentences for *can* and *can't*. PARTNER 1. Use this page. PARTNER 2. Turn to page 52.

DIRECTIONS: First you are the speaker. Say the sentences to your partner. The vowels of *can* or *can't* and the rhythm of your sentence help your partner understand.

1. My friends can't help you.
2. This man can't fix the TV.
3. I can finish this book today.
4. She can find the word in the dictionary.
5. He can't drive a truck.
6. We can call you later.

Now you are the listener. Your partner will say some sentences with *can* or *can't*. Circle the word you hear in the sentence. Number 7 is an example.

7. I ______ reach the book on the shelf.
   a. can b. (can't)
8. They ______ find their keys.
   a. can b. can't
9. You ______ use this phone.
   a. can b. can't
10. The mailman ______ leave a package.
    a. can b. can't
11. We ______ give you a ride.
    a. can b. can't
12. He ______ answer the question.
    a. can b. can't

Now compare answers with your partner.

6. INTERVIEW. Pair Practice for Sentence Stress and Rhythm with *can* and *can't*.

DIRECTIONS: Use the cues to interview a partner. You can take notes to help you remember your partner's answers.

EXAMPLE:
(CUE): . . . read Chinese?
YOU: Can you read Chinese?

Your partner will interview you, too. Choose who will ask or answer first. After the interviews, tell the other students in the class about the things your partner *can* and *can't* do. You can use your notes. When you speak to the class about your partner, do not stress *can*. Negative words are stressed, so you need to stress *can't*.

EXAMPLE:
Kim can cook eggs. Kim can't read Chinese.

CUES
1. . . . write backwards?
2. . . . draw beautiful pictures?
3. . . . play the piano?
4. . . . lift a hundred pounds?
5. . . . fix a TV?
6. . . . use a computer?

7. REPORT. Class Practice for Sentence Stress and Rhythm in Negative Sentences.

DIRECTIONS: On a sheet of paper, make two lists. Write five things you did last weekend. Then write five things you did not do last weekend. After you finish your list, use your list to tell the class about last weekend. Speak in complete sentences. Use stress and unstress to practice English rhythm.

PART FIVE Stress In *wh*- Questions

A *wh*- question begins with a *wh*- word. Here are some examples of *wh*- words: *who, where, how,* and *when*. Can you think of other *wh*- words?

PRACTICE ACTIVITIES

1. LISTENING DISCRIMINATION.

DIRECTIONS: Listen to the *wh*- questions. Mark the stressed syllables and words. Blacken the dots.

EXAMPLE:

● o o ●o
Where are you going?

1. What's his name?
2. How do you do it?
3. Where's my red jacket?
4. When does class start?
5. Why are you crying?
6. How much does it cost?
7. What do you think?
8. Where do you go to school?

FIGURE IT OUT

Which new words are stressed in the *wh*- questions? Write a rule.

RULE FOR *WH*- QUESTION WORDS

Wh- question words *(how, what, where)* are *(circle one)* stressed not stressed.

Now turn to page 39. Put this information on your chart "Summary of Stressed and Unstressed Words in Sentences."

2. READ ALOUD.

DIRECTIONS: Now read the *wh*- questions above. Say the stressed words high, long, and loud.

3. SPEAKING. Pair or Group Practice Pictures for Stress in *wh-* Questions and Rhythm.

DIRECTIONS: Below are pictures of people, their names, ages, and professions. Each person lives in an American city. Take turns asking and answering questions about the people. Stress your questions and answers correctly.

EXAMPLE:

STUDENT 1: I'd like to know about John.
STUDENT 2: OK.
STUDENT 1: What's John's last name?
STUDENT 2: Benson.
STUDENT 1: How old is he?
STUDENT 2: He's 23.
STUDENT 1: What does he do?
STUDENT 2: He's a teacher.
STUDENT 1: Where does he live?
STUDENT 2: He lives in New York.

KEN
Last name: White
Age: 31
Profession: architect
From: Houston

JOY
Last name: Goldman
Age: 30
Profession: nurse
From: Denver

JOHN
Last name: Benson
Age: 23
Profession: teacher
From: New York

EMMA
Last name: Stevens
Age: 19
Profession: teller
From: Philadelphia

MARK
Last name: Peterson
Age: 54
Profession: dentist
From: Washington, D.C.

LIZ
Last name: Bennett
Age: 26
Profession: designer
From: Chicago

SCOTT
Last name: Kim
Age: 27
Profession: pilot
From: Honolulu

WANDA
Last name: Silvers
Age: 20
Profession: movie star
From: Los Angeles

RAY
Last name: Moore
Age: 40
Profession: letter carrier
From: Boston

VICKY
Last name: Lee
Age: 34
Profession: doctor
From: Baltimore

FRED
Last name: Jackson
Age: 59
Profession: engineer
From: Atlanta

ISABEL
Last name: Fay
Age: 51
Profession: travel agent
From: Memphis

4. SPEAKING. Hobbies and Interests. Guided Conversation to Practice Stress in *wh-* Questions and Rhythm.

DIRECTIONS: Here are a list of free-time activities and a list of places. Take turns asking and answering questions. Stress *wh-* questions and sentences correctly.

EXAMPLE:

FRIEND 1: What do you like to do in your free time?

FRIEND 2: I like to ride horses.

FRIEND 1: Where do you ride horses?

FRIEND 2: I usually ride horses at the park.

FREE-TIME ACTIVITIES		PLACES
play soccer	go jogging	at the park
ride horses	go to the movies	at the beach
play cards	listen to music	at home
read books	watch TV	at school
go fishing	play tennis	out of town
play golf		in the neighborhood

MODEL CONVERSATION

FRIEND 1: What do you like to do in your free time?
FRIEND 2: I like to ____________________ .
FRIEND 1: Where do you ____________________ ?
FRIEND 2: I usually ______________ ________________ .

PARTNER 1

5a. LISTENING DISCRIMINATION AND SPEAKING. American Holidays. Pair Practice for *wh-* Questions and Rhythm. PARTNER 1. Use this page. PARTNER 2. Turn to page 52.

DIRECTIONS: How much does your partner know about American holidays? First ask some questions. Your partner will answer with a short phrase. Repeat any questions your partner does not understand. If your partner answers wrong or does not know the answer, say the answer.

EXAMPLE: Memorial Day (in the month of May)

YOU: When's Memorial Day?
YOUR PARTNER: In the month of May.
YOU: That's right. When's . . .

1. Thanksgiving (in the month of November)
2. Lincoln's Birthday (in the month of February)
3. Labor Day (in the month of September)
4. Father's Day (in the month of June)
5. Christmas (in the month of December)

Now listen to your partner's questions. Answer with the phrase *in the month of* and then say the answer. Stress the noun in the phrase and the correct syllable of the month. If you do not know the answer, your partner will tell you.

EXAMPLE:

YOUR PARTNER: When's Memorial Day?
YOU: In the month of May.
YOUR PARTNER: That's right. When's . . .

6. INTERVIEW. Getting to Know You. Pair Practice for Stress in *wh-* Questions and Rhythm.

DIRECTIONS: For this interview, choose your partner. Create five *wh-* questions. Use them to interview your partner. You can take notes to help you remember your partner's answers. Your partner will interview you, too. Choose who will ask or answer first. After the interviews, tell the other students in the class about your partner. You can use your notes.

1.

2.

3.

4.

5.

PARTNER 2

6b. LISTENING DISCRIMINATION AND SPEAKING. Where Is It? Pair Practice.

PARTNER 2. Use this page. PARTNER 1. Turn to page 37.

DIRECTIONS: First listen to your partner's questions. Use one of the phrases from the list to answer. Stress the noun in the phrase. Ask your partner to repeat any questions you do not understand.

PHRASES

in a bank
on a bench
in the hall
at the park
in my room
at a store
in the yard

Now ask some questions. Your partner will answer with a short phrase. Repeat any questions your partner does not understand.

8. Where did you sleep?
9. Where did you learn that word?
10. Where did you leave your pen?
11. Where did you work?
12. Where did you play handball?
13. Where did you put your coat?
14. Where did you buy your hat?

PAIR PRACTICE: Partner 2

PARTNER 2

9b. LISTENING DISCRIMINATION AND SPEAKING. Pair Practice Sentence Completion.
PARTNER 2. Use this page. PARTNER 1. Turn to page 41.

DIRECTIONS: First listen to your partner's phrases. Use the phrases to create a sentence. You can use the phrase in any part of your sentence.

EXAMPLE:	YOUR PARTNER:	at the bank
	YOU:	I saw my instructor at the bank.
	Or:	The teller at the bank was polite.
	Or:	I opened an account at the bank.

Stress the correct syllables and words in your sentences.

Now say some phrases to your partner. Stress the phrases correctly. Your partner needs to create a complete sentence from each phrase. Repeat any phrases your partner does not understand.

EXAMPLE:	YOU:	by the sofa
	YOUR PARTNER:	The table by the sofa has a drawer.
	Or:	He can find my notebook by the sofa.
	Or:	Let's put these lamps by the sofa.

8. in the park
9. on Friday
10. at the movies
11. in a restaurant
12. to my best friend
13. at night
14. in class on Monday

PARTNER 2

1b. SPEAKING AND LISTENING. Pair Practice for Stress, Unstress, and Rhythm.
PARTNER 2. Use this page. PARTNER 1. Turn to page 42.

DIRECTIONS: Tom is having a party. You have a list of things Tom needs. Your partner has a list, too. You want to know all the things on Tom's list. Take turns asking and answering questions to complete your list. Stress the nouns and verbs in your answers. Do not stress the articles and prepositions.

EXAMPLE:	YOU:	Does Tom still need potato chips?
	YOUR PARTNER:	Yes, he needs a bag of potato chips. Does Tom still need Coke?
	YOU:	Yes, he needs twelve cans of Coke. Does . . .

TOM'S PARTY LIST

a loaf of bread	a package of candy
____________ cheese	a jar of pickles
a bag of popcorn	a bag of peanuts
____________ pretzels	____________ juice
twelve cans of Coke	a carton of milk
a bag of potato chips	____________ napkins
____________ cookies	____________ balloons

PARTNER 2

5b. LISTENING DISCRIMINATION AND SPEAKING. Pair Practice Sentences for *can* and *can't*. PARTNER 2. Use this page. PARTNER 1. Turn to page 46.

DIRECTIONS: First you are the listener. Your partner will say some sentences with *can* or *can't*. Circle the word you hear in the sentence. Number 1 is an example.

1. My friends ______ help you.
   a. can b. (can't)
2. This man ______ fix the TV.
   a. can b. can't
3. I ______ finish this book today.
   a. can b. can't
4. She ______ find the word in the dictionary.
   a. can b. can't
5. He ______ drive a truck.
   a. can b. can't
6. We ______ call you later.
   a. can b. can't

Now you are the speaker. Say the sentences to your partner. The vowels of *can* or *can't* and the rhythm of your sentence helps your partner understand.

7. I can't reach the book on the shelf.
8. They can't find their keys.
9. You can use this phone.
10. The mailman can leave a package.
11. We can give you a ride.
12. He can answer the question.

Now compare answers with your partner.

PARTNER 2

5b. LISTENING DISCRIMINATION AND SPEAKING. American Holidays. Pair Practice for *wh-* Questions and Rhythm. PARTNER 2. Use this page. PARTNER 1. Turn to page 49.

DIRECTIONS: Your partner wants to find out how much you know about American holidays. Answer with the phrase *in the month of* and then say the answer. Stress the noun in the phrase and the correct syllable of the month. If you do not know the answer, your partner will tell you.

EXAMPLE:	YOUR PARTNER:	When's Memorial Day?
	YOU:	In the month of May.
	YOUR PARTNER:	That's right. When's . . .

Now, how much does your partner know about American holidays? Ask some questions. Your partner will answer with a short phrase. Repeat any questions your partner does not understand. If your partner answers wrong or does not know the answer, say the answer.

EXAMPLE:	Memorial Day (in the month of May)	
	YOU:	When's Memorial Day?
	YOUR PARTNER:	In the month of May.
	YOU:	That's right. When's . . .

6. Mother's Day (in the month of May)
7. Halloween (in the month of October)
8. Washington's Birthday (in the month of February)
9. Flag Day (in the month of June)
10. Independence Day (in the month of July)

Sentence Stress, Rhythm Groups, and Linking

LESSON 6

In Lesson 5 you learned about sentence stress. Regular stresses make rhythm. Now you are going to learn about sounds in rhythm groups.

PART ONE Rhythm Groups

Sentences and questions usually have some unstressed syllables and some stressed syllables.

 Listen to these short sentences:

He had a bad dream.

My watch is broken.

Stan's wearing his glasses.

I can't remember her address.

In long sentences, we say syllables and words in groups.

 Listen to these long sentences:

The man at the desk / was asking us questions.

Three new students / came to class today.

I met my best friend / on a plane.

Her parents / are going to send her / some more money.

These groups of words are rhythm groups. There are one or more stressed syllables in each group.

PRACTICE ACTIVITIES

1. READ ALOUD.

DIRECTIONS: Read the four short sentences on page 53. Then read the four long sentences on page 53. Say the stressed syllables and words long and loud.

2. READ ALOUD.

DIRECTIONS: Here are some long sentences. Practice reading them in rhythm groups.

1. The first man in line / is paying in cash.
2. We ran out of gas / at Sixth and Green Streets.
3. Please leave your umbrella / outside the door.
4. The doctor and nurse / can see you soon.
5. The instructor told us / to finish our homework.
6. The bookstore on campus / is open till eight.
7. He likes to read / and he loves to cook.
8. You can write your name / at the top of the page.
9. They made an appointment / to see the advisor / on Monday.
10. After the concert, / we went to a restaurant / to have dessert.

3. LISTENING DISCRIMINATION.

DIRECTIONS: You are going to hear some long sentences. Put a line (/) between the rhythm groups you hear.

EXAMPLE:

Lin's parents / are coming this weekend.

1. Dogs and cats make good pets.
2. Our last class is on Friday the 10th.
3. The food in that restaurant is always good.
4. You don't need a pen to take this exam.
5. She likes to sit in the back of the room.
6. She put down her book and answered the phone.
7. My favorite class is at eight in the morning.
8. He's writing a story about life in his country.
9. Ted found your wallet under a desk in Room 9.
10. The police and fireman are helping the victims.

Now read the ten long sentences. Practice reading them in rhythm groups.

4. SPEAKING. Pair or Group Practice for Rhythm Groups. Below is a picture of Joe's room. Joe is very messy. Joe is strange, too.

DIRECTIONS: Take turns making sentences about Joe's room. Use rhythm groups in your sentences.

EXAMPLE:

STUDENT 1: Joe's crazy! His alarm clock / is under his shoe / on the floor.
STUDENT 2: I know. Joe's messy! His socks are / on the chair / on top of his books.
STUDENT 3: I know. Joe's crazy! His notebook is / on the bed / next to his pillow.

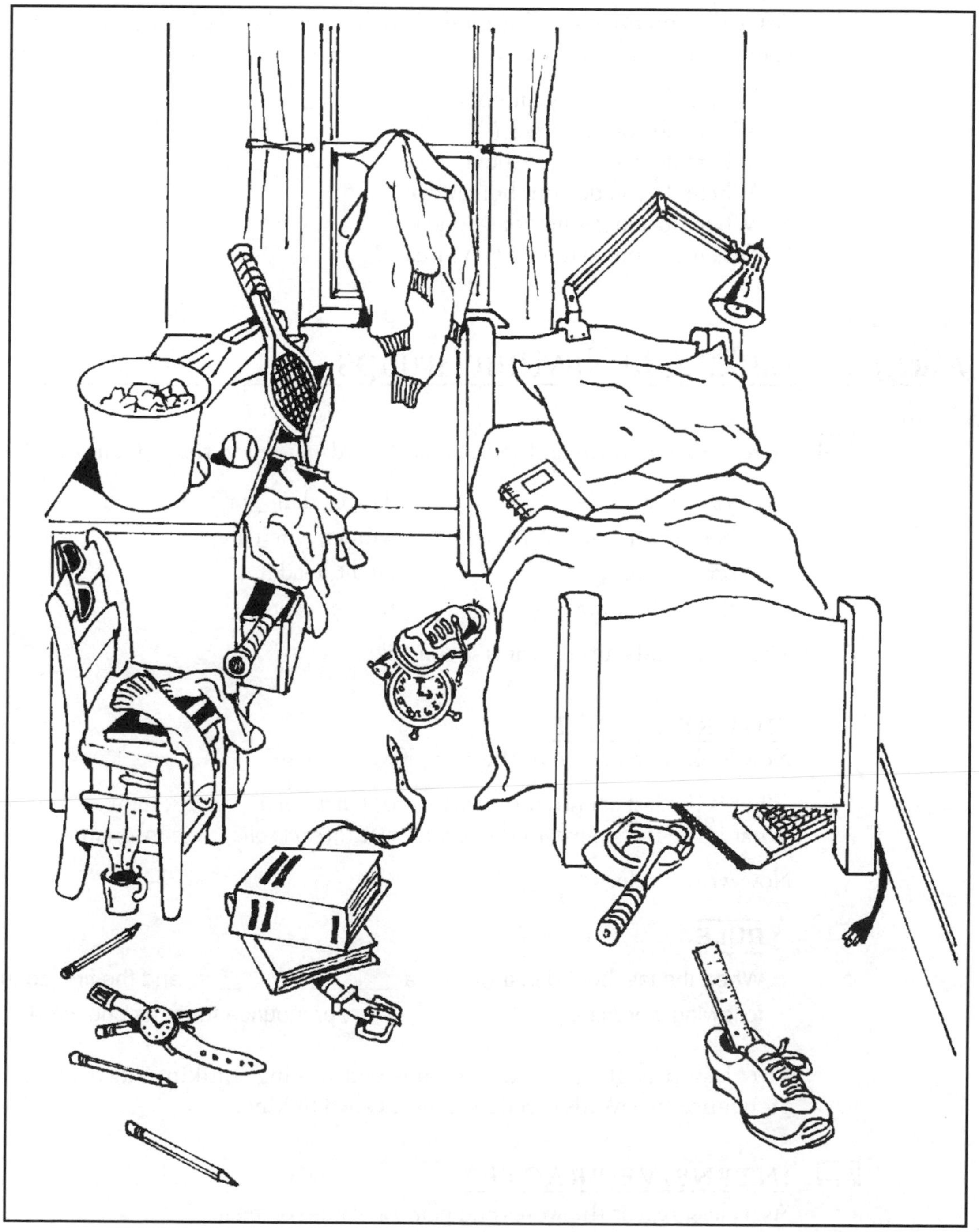

5. INTERVIEW. Pair Practice for Sentence Stress and Rhythm Groups.

DIRECTIONS: Interview a partner with the questions below. You can take notes to help you remember your partner's answers. Your partner will interview you, too. Choose who will ask or answer first.

Answer the questions with rhythm groups.

EXAMPLE:

YOUR PARTNER: Where do you buy your food?
YOU: I buy my food / at a store on the corner.

After the interviews, tell the other students in the class about your partner. You can use your notes. When you speak to the class about your partner, use rhythm groups.

1. Where do you buy your books?
2. Where do you eat lunch?
3. Where do you like to study?
4. Where do you do your homework?
5. When do you get up / on Mondays?
6. When do you go to bed / on Fridays?

PART TWO Linking In Rhythm Groups

Here are some words and some pairs of words. Listen to them. Compare them.

visit, is it
butter, what are
service, serve us
flower, how are
dancer, dance or
winner, when are
credit, read it
notice, wrote us

The words and pairs of words sound alike.

FIGURE IT OUT

Now look at and listen to the pairs of words again.

What is the last sound in the first word? *(circle one)* consonant vowel
What is the first sound in the second word? *(circle one)* consonant vowel

Now write a rule.

RULE

When the last sound in a word is a ________________ and the first sound in the following word is a ________________, pronounce them as one word.

This lesson is about rhythm groups and linking. Linking means to put together. You pronounce two words together. This is called **linking.**

INTENSIVE PRACTICE

As a class, repeat the words and pairs of words you hear.

EXAMPLE:

cup, look up

PRACTICE ACTIVITIES

1. READ ALOUD.

DIRECTIONS: Practice linking consonants to vowels.

/s/
It's easy.
I have lots of friends.
Let's eat lunch.

/z/
He's angry.
She's in trouble.
Where's our car?

/m/
Am I too late?
Please come in.
What time is it?

/n/
You can ask later.
He's an engineer.
Turn off the TV.

/r/
They're in class.
Our exam was long.
Your answer is right.

/l/
She can tell us.
Fill out this application.
He's as tall as you.

/p/
It's on top of the desk.
Keep up the good work.
I'll have a cup of coffee.

/t/
They get up late.
Class starts at eight.
Please put it away.

2. LISTENING DISCRIMINATION.

DIRECTIONS: Listen to some short sentences and questions. You are going to hear linking. Circle the letter of the sentence or question you hear.

EXAMPLE:
Where is it?
a. When is it? (b.) Where is it?

1.	a. She does it.	b. She did it.
2.	a. Where are they?	b. What are they?
3.	a. We show it.	b. We showed it.
4.	a. They make us glad.	b. They made us glad.
5.	a. When are we going?	b. Where are we going?
6.	a. I had lots of fun.	b. I had a lot of fun.
7.	a. He has our number.	b. He had our number.
8.	a. Don't take it.	b. Don't tape it.
9.	a. There's our family.	b. They're our family.
10.	a. Can she speak up?	b. Can she speed up?

3. LISTENING DISCRIMINATION.

DIRECTIONS: Listen to the short sentences. Underline linked words you hear. There is one link in each short sentence.

EXAMPLE:

It's only a game.

1. He gave us some paper.
2. She explained their idea.
3. His answer was right.
4. Have this glass of water.
5. Keep on doing the work.
6. It's easy to do.
7. All of the students came.
8. I want to have some examples.
9. Please drive us to the store.
10. Don't leave any money here.

Now read the ten sentences. Link two words in each sentence.

You link words in the same rhythm group in long sentences. You do not link words between rhythm groups.

EXAMPLES:

They sold us a car / in October.

When I was a child, / I was afraid of the dark.

4. READ ALOUD.

DIRECTIONS: Here are some phrases and long sentences. Practice linking in rhythm groups.

1. students ate, in a

   The students ate in a cafeteria.
2. was amazed, hear about it

   I was amazed to hear about it.
3. plane arrives, this afternoon

   His plane arrives this afternoon.
4. told us, an interesting

   She told us an interesting story.
5. can open it, take all of

   You can open it and take all of them.
6. stop at, for a

   Please stop at the store for a newspaper.
7. put on, look at

   I put on my glasses to look at this.
8. some ice, glass of

   Here's some ice for your glass of water.
9. women are, some information

   These women are waiting for some information.
10. there's an apartment, on a

    There's an apartment for rent on a quiet street.

PARTNER 1

5a. LISTENING DISCRIMINATION AND SPEAKING. What Is It? Pair Practice for Linking. PARTNER 1. Use this page. PARTNER 2. Turn to page 60.

DIRECTIONS: First say some sentences. Link words in your sentences. Then ask your partner, "What is it?" Your partner is going to answer with a short sentence.

EXAMPLE:

YOU:	It's a room on top of a house under a roof. What is it?
YOUR PARTNER:	I know what it is. It's an attic.

1. It's a place. You can see some airplanes there. What is it?
2. It's a thing made of cloth. You need it when it rains. What is it?
3. It's a round, red fruit. What is it?
4. It's a part of your body. A hand is at the end. What is it?
5. It's made of water. It's very big. It's bigger than a lake or sea. What is it?
6. It's a machine. It takes people to the top of a building. What is it?

Now listen to your partner's sentences. Your partner is going to describe something. Say "I know what it is." Then use a word from the list to answer. Link words in your answer.

EXAMPLE:

YOUR PARTNER:	It's a group of people. They carry guns and fight. What is it?
YOU:	I know what it is. It's an army.

WORDS

actor	envelope
airplane	office
egg	orange

6. LISTEN AND REPORT. Local Movies.

DIRECTIONS: Look at the movie section in a newspaper. Find an ad for a theater in your town or neighborhood. Look at the telephone number and call the theater on the phone. Listen to a recorded message about the movies. On a sheet of paper, write the names of the movies and the times they are playing. You can listen to the recorded message more than one time to get your information.

Next, tell the class what movies are playing. Tell them the times, too. You can use your notes. Use rhythm groups and linking when you talk to the class.

PARTNER 2

5b. LISTENING DISCRIMINATION AND SPEAKING. What Is It? Pair Practice for Linking. PARTNER 2. Use this page. PARTNER 1. Turn to page 59.

DIRECTIONS: First listen to your partner's sentences. Your partner is going to describe something. Say, "I know what it is." Then use a word from the list to answer. Link words in your answer.

EXAMPLE:

YOUR PARTNER: It's a room on top of a house under a roof. What is it?
YOU: I know what it is. It's an attic.

WORDS

airport	elevator
arm	ocean
apple	umbrella

Now say some sentences. Link words in your sentences. Then ask your partner, "What is it?" Your partner is going to answer with a short sentence.

EXAMPLE:

YOU: It's a group of people. They carry guns and fight. What is it?
YOUR PARTNER: I know what it is. It's an army.

7. It's a place. People work at desks there. What is it?
8. It's a machine for travel. You fly in it. What is it?
9. It's made of paper. You put a letter in it. What is it?
10. It's a round, orange fruit. What is it?
11. It's a person. He plays in a movie. What is it?
12. It's oval and white. We can eat it for breakfast. What is it?

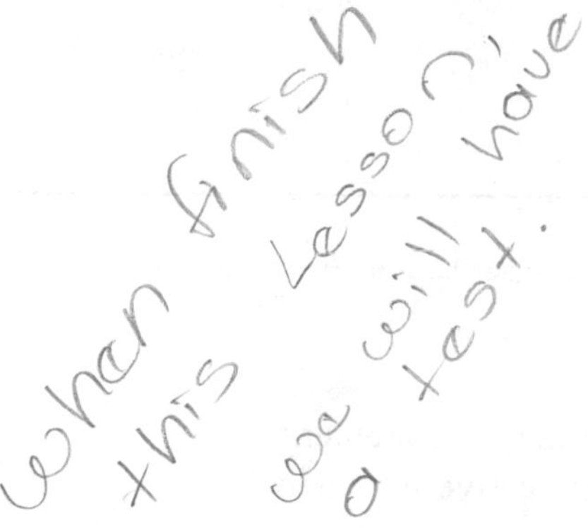

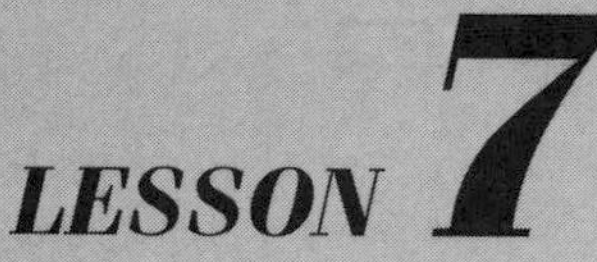

Rising/Falling Intonation

There are generally three tones in an English sentence or question. The tones are like musical notes.

high ______________________________
medium ______________________________
low ______________________________

Here is an English sentence. Listen to the tones.

EXAMPLE:

high ______________ **stu** ______________
medium ________ **He's a** ______________
low ______________________ **dent.** ________

The sentence starts on the medium tone. Then it rises to the high tone. Last, it falls to the low tone. This is **rising/falling intonation.** This book shows rising/falling intonation like this:

He's a student. He came to class on Monday.

Here is an English question. Listen to the tones.

EXAMPLE:

high ______________ **busy?** ______________
medium ________ **Are you** ______________
low ______________________________

The question starts on the medium tone. Then it rises to the high tone. This is **rising intonation.** This book shows rising intonation like this:

Are you busy? Do you need some help?

This lesson is about stressed words and rising/falling intonation in sentences and questions.

PART ONE Statements

A **statement** is a negative or affirmative sentence. A statement is *not* a question.

Look at and listen to the examples:

I worked all day yesterday. (affirmative statement)
They can't hear the question. (negative statement)

You will learn about intonation and statements.

PRACTICE ACTIVITIES

1. LISTENING DISCRIMINATION.

DIRECTIONS: Listen to these statements. Circle the letter of the intonation you hear.

EXAMPLE:

They're going home. (a.) ↗↘ b. ↗

1. She's very pretty. (a.) ↗↘ b. ↗
2. It isn't raining. (a.) ↗↘ b. ↗
3. The movie was boring. (a.) ↗↘ b. ↗
4. I don't have a ruler. (a.) ↗↘ b. ↗
5. They can't answer. (a.) ↗↘ b. ↗
6. The race is starting. (a.) ↗↘ b. ↗

FIGURE IT OUT

What intonation do you use in statements? Write a rule.

RULE FOR AFFIRMATIVE AND NEGATIVE STATEMENTS

Affirmative and negative statements have *(circle one)* rising/falling rising intonation.

Now listen to the statements again and repeat them. The last word in each statement has two syllables. Where does the the tone rise? Where does the tone fall? Write a rule.

RULE FOR RISING AND FALLING TONES

The tone rises on the ________ stressed syllable of a statement. The tone falls after the ________ stressed syllable of a statement.

2. READ ALOUD.

DIRECTIONS: Now read the statements above. Use rising/falling intonation.

3. LISTENING DISCRIMINATION.

DIRECTIONS: Listen to the short sentences. Put a dot over the stressed syllables and words.

EXAMPLE:

I gave him my number. (dots over "I" and "num-")

1. Our plane was early.
2. It starts on Friday.
3. She wants to play tennis.
4. The bookstore isn't open.
5. I don't like coffee.
6. They need to tell you.
7. We forgot to ask them.
8. He doesn't want to buy it.

4. READ ALOUD.

DIRECTIONS: Look at the statements again. Use your Rule for Rising and Falling Tones. Figure out which syllables or words rise and fall. Then read the statements aloud.

EXAMPLE: I gave him my number.

5. LISTENING DISCRIMINATION.

DIRECTIONS: Listen to these statements. Each statement has stress on the last syllable.

1. He feels sad.
2. It's time to go home.
3. They can't spell the word.
4. She didn't know my name.
5. Lisa wants to take a class.
6. We don't get up at eight.

The last stress is the last syllable in the statement. Make the tone on the last stress rise. Make the tone on the last stress fall, too. Make the tone *rise* and *fall* on the *same* syllable.

Now listen to the statements again and repeat them. Practice making the tone rise and fall on the same syllable.

EXAMPLE: He feels sad.

6. READ ALOUD.

DIRECTIONS: Read these statements. Practice making the tone rise and fall on the same syllable.

1. The work was boring and hard.
2. Last year she lived in Spain.
3. He didn't take a vacation in June.
4. Our office is on the first floor.
5. We practice for an hour each day.
6. I did well on the quiz and the test.
7. You can't eat and drink in this room.
8. Joe doesn't really understand.

7. READ ALOUD.

DIRECTIONS: Here are some statements. Some statements have stress on the last syllable and some statements do *not*. Use your Rule for Rising and Falling Tones. Figure out which syllables or words rise or fall.

EXAMPLE:

Henry comes to campus on foot.

1. The lab isn't open on Sunday.
2. They're going to work by bus.
3. The books for my class are expensive.
4. She talked on the phone for an hour.
5. The instructor didn't give us homework.
6. You don't need a ball for the game.
7. There aren't any dishes on the table.
8. At night we can listen to music.
9. Summer classes are going to start in May.
10. We didn't want to tell him the news.

Now read these statements aloud.

8. SPEAKING. Guided Conversation to Practice Rising/Falling Intonation.

DIRECTIONS: Here is a list of topics. With a partner, take turns talking about things you like. Use rising/falling intonation in your statements.

EXAMPLE:

STUDENT 1: My favorite day of the week is Saturday.

STUDENT 2: That's interesting. My favorite day of the week is Tuesday.

TOPICS

color	hobby	TV program	season
food	holiday	day of the week	place to have fun
sport	place to study	kind of movie	kind of music

9. REPORT.

DIRECTIONS: Use the information from section 8 above to tell the class about your partner. Use rising/falling intonation in your report.

EXAMPLE: My partner is Mario. His favorite color is red. His favorite . . .

10. ROLE-PLAY. What Do You Look Like? Pair Practice for Rising/Falling Intonation.

DIRECTIONS: Imagine one student in your pair is Sue's friend. The other student is Todd's friend. You are on the phone. You do not know what your partner looks like. Sue and Todd want you and your partner to meet at the library. Use the cues to find out what your partner looks like.

EXAMPLE:

TODD'S FRIEND: My name's Chang.
SUE'S FRIEND: My name's Emi. I can meet you at ten o'clock. What do you look like?
TODD'S FRIEND: I'm 5 feet 10 inches tall. I have short black hair . . . What do you look like?
SUE'S FRIEND: I'm 5 feet 4 inches tall. I have . . .

CUES

tall	hair color	weight	glasses
hair length	eye color	age	clothing

MODEL CONVERSATION

TODD'S FRIEND: My name's ______________.
SUE'S FRIEND: My name's ______________ . I can meet you at ________ o'clock. What do you look like?
TODD'S FRIEND: I'm . . . What do you look like?
SUE'S FRIEND: I'm . . .
TODD'S FRIEND: OK. I'll see you at ________ o'clock. Bye!

PART TWO Commands

A **command** is a sentence. A command can be negative or affirmative. A command orders or tells a person to do something.

Look at and listen to the examples:

Take your shoes off. (affirmative command)
Don't lose your keys. (negative command)

You will learn about intonation and commands.

PRACTICE ACTIVITIES

1. LISTENING DISCRIMINATION.

DIRECTIONS: Listen to the commands. Circle the letter of the intonation you hear.

EXAMPLE:

Set the table. (a.) ↗↘ b. ↗

1. Don't forget. a. ↗↘ b. ↗
2. Put on your jacket. a. ↗↘ b. ↗
3. Tell us a story. a. ↗↘ b. ↗
4. Don't order dessert. a. ↗↘ b. ↗
5. Don't buy a paper. a. ↗↘ b. ↗
6. Give us your number. a. ↗↘ b. ↗
7. Don't answer. a. ↗↘ b. ↗
8. Leave a message. a. ↗↘ b. ↗

FIGURE IT OUT

What intonation do you use in commands? What intonation do you use in negative commands? Write a rule.

RULE FOR COMMANDS AND NEGATIVE COMMANDS

Commands and negative commands have *(circle one)* rising/falling rising intonation.

Now listen to the commands again and repeat them. The last word in each command has two syllables. Where does the tone rise? Where does the tone fall? Write a rule.

RULE FOR RISING AND FALLING TONES

The tone rises on the ________ stressed syllable of a command. The tone falls after the ________ stressed syllable of a command.

2. READ ALOUD.

DIRECTIONS: Now read the commands above. Use rising/falling intonation.

3. LISTENING DISCRIMINATION.

DIRECTIONS: Listen to these short commands. Put a dot over the stressed syllables and words.

EXAMPLE: Give them some money.

1. Don't call too early.
2. Take it to the concert.
3. Write her a letter.
4. Don't leave it open.
5. Tell him you're sorry.
6. Move the chair and table.
7. Don't try to do it.
8. Don't let her follow.

4. READ ALOUD.

DIRECTIONS: Look at the commands again. Use your Rule for Rising and Falling Tones. Figure out which syllables or words rise and fall. Then read the commands aloud.

EXAMPLE: Give them some money.

5. LISTENING DISCRIMINATION.

DIRECTIONS: Listen to the commands. Each command has stress on the last syllable.

1. Put the book here.
2. Don't be late.
3. Spell your name.
4. Don't forget your hat.
5. Put your bags in the car.
6. Don't wait for the train.
7. Don't drop that glass.
8. Lend him your pen.

The last stress is the last syllable in the command. Like statements, you need to make the tone *rise* and *fall* on the *same* syllable.

Now listen to the commands again and repeat them. Practice making the tone rise and fall on the same syllable.

EXAMPLE: Put the book here.

6. READ ALOUD.

DIRECTIONS: Read the commands below. Practice making the tone rise and fall on the same syllable.

1. Answer it now.
2. Show me your card.
3. Try to take a class next spring.
4. Walk up the street on the left.
5. Don't forget your notes for the test.
6. Don't try to move that desk.
7. Leave your notebooks in the room.
8. Don't park my car on the street.

7. READ ALOUD.

DIRECTIONS: Here are some commands. Some commands have stress on the last syllable and some commands do *not*. Use your Rule for Rising and Falling Tones. Figure out which syllables or words rise and fall.

EXAMPLE: Say the word loudly.

1. Read the report by Monday.
2. Finish your test at seven.
3. Don't buy any tapes at that store.
4. Put your name and address on the card.
5. Drive Mohan and Shah to the airport.
6. Put two coins in here for the washer.
7. Pronounce these words correctly.
8. Don't write on the front of my book.
9. Bring her some aspirin and some water.

Now read the commands aloud.

8. SPEAKING. Guided Conversation to Practice Rising/Falling Intonation in Commands.

DIRECTIONS: Here is the inside of a house and a list of furniture. Imagine you are moving into the house. Take turns as the home owner and the mover. Use rising/falling intonation in your commands.

EXAMPLE:

MOVER: Tell me where to put the big lamp.

HOME OWNER: Please put the big lamp in the living room.

MOVER: OK. Tell me where to . . .

FURNITURE

sofa	dresser	bed
table	desk	big chair
big lamp	bookshelf	nightstand
small lamp	mirror	TV
small chairs	stereo	end table

MODEL CONVERSATION

MOVER: Tell me where to put the ___________.

HOME OWNER: Please put the ____________ in the __________.

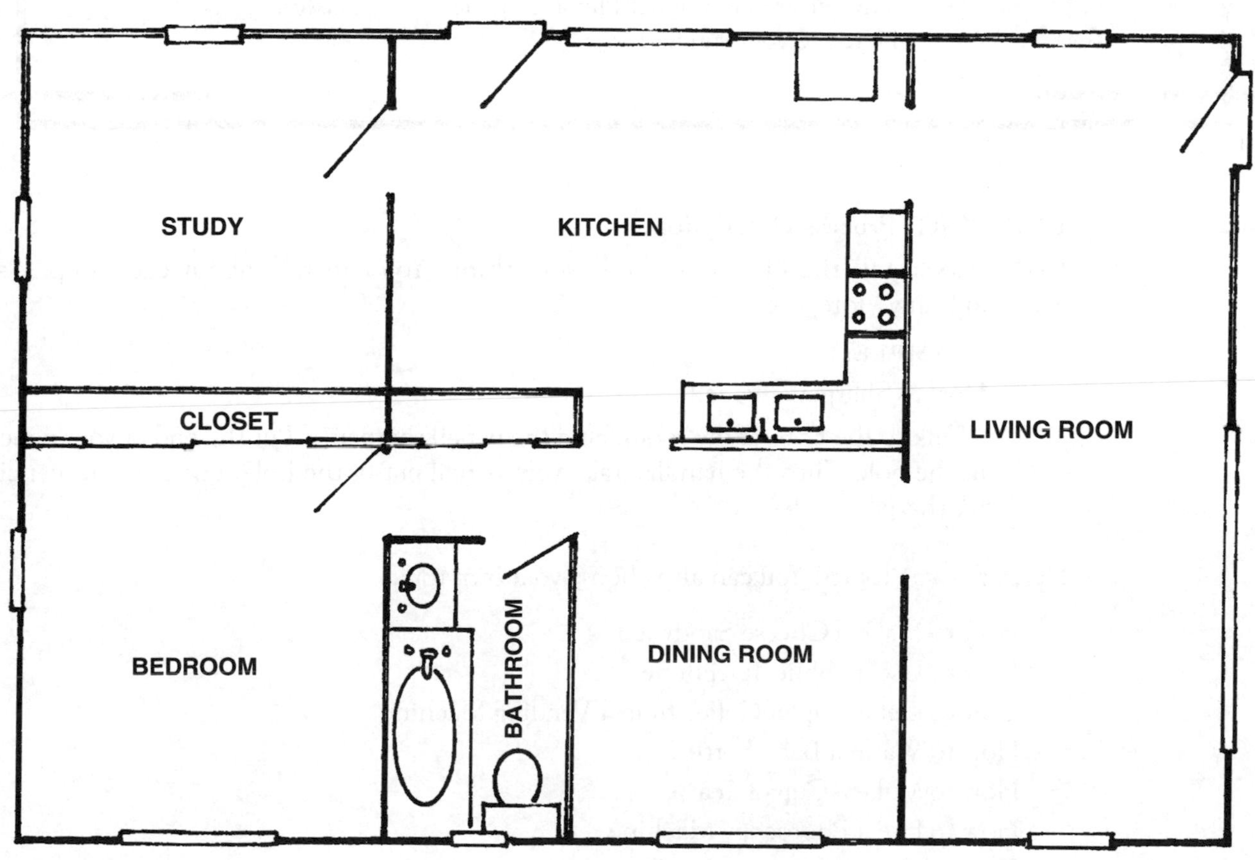

PARTNER 1

9a. LISTENING DISCRIMINATION AND SPEAKING. Pair Practice for Rising/Falling Intonation in Commands and Statements. PARTNER 1. Use this page. PARTNER 2. Turn to page 74.

DIRECTIONS: Imagine you and your partner are on vacation together. First say the short statements and create polite commands with the words in parentheses ( ).

EXAMPLE:

The sun is very bright! (give me)
YOU: The sun is very bright! Please give me my sunglasses.
YOUR PARTNER: Here are your sunglasses.

1. I don't have my watch. (tell me)
2. I have a headache. (give me)
3. I'm cold. (give me)
4. It's hot in here! (open)
5. I want to buy a T-shirt. (lend me)
6. I want to hear music. (turn on)
7. I'm lost! (show me)

Now listen to your partner's statements and commands. Then create a response.

EXAMPLE:

YOUR PARTNER: The sun is very bright! Please give me my sunglasses.
YOU: Here are your sunglasses.

10. REPORT. Process Description.

DIRECTIONS: Tell the class how to do something. You can talk about each step. Use commands in your report.

EXAMPLE:

How to Sharpen a Pencil

"Walk to the back of the room. Find the pencil sharpener. Put the end of your pencil in the hole. Turn the handle. Take your pencil out of the hole. Look at your pencil. It's sharp."

Here are some topics. You can also choose your own topic.

How to Make a Cheese Sandwich
How to Use a Public Telephone
How to Get a Cup of Coffee from a Vending Machine
How to Warm a Baby Bottle
How to Make a Cup of Tea
How to Use a Photocopy Machine
How to Draw a Circle with a Compass
How to Change a Flat Tire

PART THREE *wh-* Questions

In Lesson 5 on page 47, you learned about sentence stress in *wh-* questions. A *wh-* question can be negative or affirmative.

Look at and listen to the examples:

> Where are you going? (affirmative *wh-* question)
> Why don't you remember? (negative *wh-* question)

Now you will learn about intonation in *wh-* questions.

PRACTICE ACTIVITIES

1. LISTENING DISCRIMINATION.

DIRECTIONS: Listen to the *wh-* questions. Circle the letter of the intonation you hear.

EXAMPLE:

What are you doing? (a.) b.

1. How are you feeling? a. b.
2. Where's the station? a. b.
3. Who asked the question? a. b.
4. Why can't they answer? a. b.
5. When does it finish? a. b.
6. Why don't we listen? a. b.
7. Who's in the kitchen? a. b.
8. How can I manage? a. b.

FIGURE IT OUT

What intonation do you use in *wh-* questions? What intonation do you use in negative *wh-* questions? Write a rule.

RULE FOR *WH-* QUESTIONS AND NEGATIVE *WH-* QUESTIONS

Wh- questions and negative *wh-* questions have *(circle one)*
rising/falling rising intonation.

Now listen to the *wh-* questions again and repeat them. The last word in each question has two syllables. Where does the the tone rise? Where does the tone fall? Write a rule.

RULE FOR RISING AND FALLING TONES

The tone rises on the ________ stressed syllable of a *wh-* question. The tone falls after the ________ stressed syllable of a *wh-* question.

2. READ ALOUD.

DIRECTIONS: Now read the *wh-* questions above. Use rising/falling intonation.

3. LISTENING DISCRIMINATION.

DIRECTIONS: Listen to the short *wh-* questions. Put a dot over the stressed syllables and words.

EXAMPLE: Where's your wallet?

1. Whose jacket is this?
2. How much time do we have?
3. What were they saying?
4. Where does she live?
5. When does the bus come?
6. How many pages did you write?
7. How did they do it?
8. What game is he playing?

4. READ ALOUD.

DIRECTIONS: Look at the *wh-* questions again. Use your Rule for Rising and Falling Tones. Figure out which syllable or word rises. Then figure out which syllable or word falls. Read the *wh-* questions aloud.

EXAMPLE: Where's your wallet?

Like statements and commands, some *wh-* questions have the last stress on the last syllable. You need to make the tone *rise* and *fall* on the *same* syllable.

5. SPEAKING. Pair or Group Practice for Rising/Falling Intonation in *wh-* Questions.

Below you see a picture of boxes with numbers. Each box has more than one object in it.

DIRECTIONS: Take turns asking and answering questions about the boxes. Use rising/falling intonation in your questions.

EXAMPLE:

STUDENT 1: How many peanuts are in box number four?
STUDENT 2: Five. How many wheels are in box number seven?
STUDENT 3: Six. How many . . .

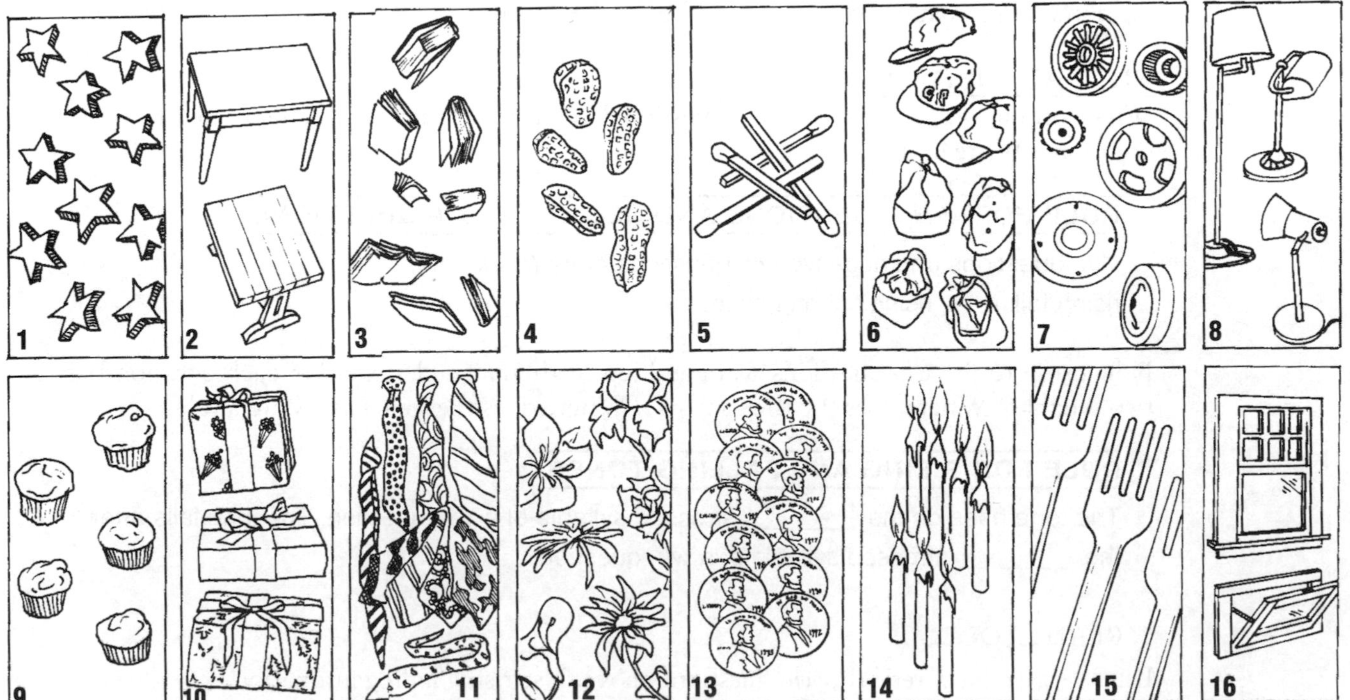

6. SPEAKING. Sightseeing in America. Guided Conversation to Practice Rising/Falling Intonation in *wh-* Questions and Statements.

DIRECTIONS: Here is a list of famous sites and places in the United States. You want to see them. Take turns asking and answering questions about the sites. Use rising/falling intonation in *wh-* questions and statements.

EXAMPLE:

PARTNER 1: What do you want to see?

PARTNER 2: I want to see the Grand Canyon.

PARTNER 1: Where's the Grand Canyon?

PARTNER 2: It's in Arizona.

SITES AND PLACES

Mount Rushmore (South Dakota)
Key West (Florida)
Niagara Falls (New York)
Mount McKinley (Alaska)
The Alamo (Texas)
Pikes Peak (Colorado)
The Grand Canyon (Arizona)
Hoover Dam (Nevada)
Death Valley (California)
The Great Salt Lake (Utah)
Plymouth Rock (Massachusetts)
Yellowstone Park (Wyoming)
Valley Forge (Pennsylvania)

MODEL CONVERSATION

PARTNER 1: What do you want to see?
PARTNER 2: I want to see ________________________.
PARTNER 1: Where's ____________________________?
PARTNER 2: It's in ________________________.

PARTNER 1

7a. LISTENING DISCRIMINATION AND SPEAKING. Pair Role-Play for Rising/Falling Intonation in *wh-* Questions. PARTNER 1. Use this page. PARTNER 2. Turn to page 74.

DIRECTIONS: You are going to travel by train. Here is a list of cities. Your partner is a ticket agent. Ask about the train schedule. Write information on the lines.

EXAMPLE:

YOU: What time is the train to Boston?
TICKET AGENT: 1:45.
YOU: What track is it on?
TICKET AGENT: Track 5.
YOU: How much is a ticket?
TICKET AGENT: $41.00 one way.
YOU: OK. Thank you.

TRAIN SCHEDULE

City	Departure	Track	Cost
Boston	*1:45*	*5*	$ *41.00*
Chicago	______	____	$______
Denver	______	____	$______
Detroit	______	____	$______
Houston	______	____	$______
Los Angeles	______	____	$______
Miami	______	____	$______
Nashville	______	____	$______
New York	______	____	$______
Washington, D.C.	______	____	$______

Now imagine you are a ticket agent at an airport. Your partner is going to travel by plane. Listen to your partner's questions and answer them. Use rising/falling intonation in your short answers.

EXAMPLE:

YOUR PARTNER: What time is the flight to Atlanta?
TICKET AGENT: 9:15.
YOUR PARTNER: What gate is it at?
TICKET AGENT: Gate 20.
YOUR PARTNER: How much is a ticket?
TICKET AGENT: $320.00 one way.
YOUR PARTNER: OK. Thank you.

SCHEDULE OF FLIGHTS

City	Departure	Gate	Cost
Honolulu	7:10	37	$499.00
Miami	8:30	14	$379.00
Atlanta	9:15	20	$320.00
New York	9:40	31	$299.00
San Francisco	10:05	28	$310.00
Dallas	10:10	19	$299.00
Cleveland	10:50	6	$189.00
Pittsburgh	11:25	23	$259.00
Chicago	11:30	12	$210.00
Denver	11:45	32	$329.00

Now compare answers with your partner.

8. INTERVIEW. Pair Practice for Rising/Falling Intonation in *wh-* Questions and Statements.

DIRECTIONS: Interview a partner about these future activities. Your partner will interview you, too. Choose who will ask or answer first.

Use the cues to ask questions.

EXAMPLE:

(CUE) . . . after class?

YOU: What are you going to do after class?

You can take notes. Notes help you remember your partner's answers. After the interview, tell the other students in the class about your partner. When you speak to the class about your partner, you need to use rising/falling intonation in your statements.

CUES

1. . . . after class?
2. . . . tomorrow?
3. . . . next weekend?
4. . . . during your next vacation?
5. . . . in December?
6. . . . next Monday?
7. . . . the day after tomorrow?

PAIR PRACTICE: Partner 2

PARTNER 2

9b. LISTENING DISCRIMINATION AND SPEAKING. Pair Practice for Rising/Falling Intonation in Commands and Statements. PARTNER 2. Use this page. PARTNER 1. Turn to page 68.

DIRECTIONS: Imagine you and your partner are on vacation together. First listen to your partner's statements and commands. Then create a response.

EXAMPLE:

YOUR PARTNER: The sun is very bright! Please give me my sunglasses.
YOU: Here are your sunglasses.

Now say the short statements and create polite commands with the words in parentheses ( ).

EXAMPLE:

The sun is very bright! (give me)
YOU: The sun is very bright! Please give me my sunglasses.
YOUR PARTNER: Here are your sunglasses.

8. It's noisy in here! (close)
9. My suitcase is heavy. (carry)
10. It's raining. (give me)
11. I want to take a picture. (give me)
12. It's dark in here! (turn on)
13. My hands are cold. (give me)
14. I want to read. (buy me)

PARTNER 2

7b. LISTENING DISCRIMINATION AND SPEAKING. Pair Role-Play for Rising/Falling Intonation in *wh-* Questions. PARTNER 2. Use this page. PARTNER 1. Turn to page 72.

DIRECTIONS: Imagine you are a ticket agent at a train station. Your partner is going to travel by train. Listen to your partner's questions and answer them. Use rising/falling intonation in your short answers.

EXAMPLE:

YOUR PARTNER: What time is the train to Boston?
TICKET AGENT: 1:45.
YOUR PARTNER: What track is it on?
TICKET AGENT: Track 5.
YOUR PARTNER: How much is a ticket?
TICKET AGENT: $41.00 one way.
YOUR PARTNER: OK. Thank you.

TRAIN SCHEDULE

City	Departure	Track	Cost
Nashville	9:15	7	$29.00
Chicago	10:08	1	$37.00
Houston	10:40	4	$48.00
Miami	10:55	3	$52.00
Washington, D.C.	11:20	10	$36.00
Denver	11:45	6	$66.00
Los Angeles	12:10	9	$73.00
New York	12:42	2	$45.00
Boston	1:45	5	$41.00
Detroit	1:50	8	$39.00

Now you are going to travel by plane. Here is a list of cities. Your partner is a ticket agent. Directions: Ask about the flight schedule. Write information on the lines.

EXAMPLE:

YOU: What time is the flight to Atlanta?

TICKET AGENT: 9:15.

YOU: What gate is it at?

TICKET AGENT: Gate 20.

YOU: How much is a ticket?

TICKET AGENT: $320.00 one way.

YOU: OK. Thank you.

SCHEDULE OF FLIGHTS

City	Departure	Gate	Cost
Atlanta	*9:15*	*20*	$*320.00*
Chicago	________	____	$______
Cleveland	________	____	$______
Dallas	________	____	$______
Denver	________	____	$______
Honolulu	________	____	$______
Miami	________	____	$______
New York	________	____	$______
Pittsburgh	________	____	$______
San Francisco	________	____	$______

Now compare answers with your partner.

LESSON 8

Rising Intonation

In Lesson 7 you learned about tones. There are generally three tones in English. They are like musical notes.

Here is an English question. Listen to the tones.

EXAMPLE:

high ______________________ **going?** ______________

medium ____________ **Is she** ______________________

low ____

The question starts on the medium tone. Then it rises to the high tone. This is a *rising* intonation. This book shows *rising* intonation like this:

Is she going? Do we finish at one?

This lesson is about stressed words and intonation in questions. The questions need *yes* or *no* for an answer. They are *not wh-* questions.

Yes/no questions can be negative or affirmative. Look at and listen to these examples:

Were they speaking English? (affirmative question)

Can't we come late? (negative question)

PRACTICE ACTIVITIES

1. LISTENING DISCRIMINATION.

DIRECTIONS: Listen to the yes/no questions. Circle the letters of the intonation you hear.

EXAMPLE: Is it a map? a. (b.)

1. Are you bored? a. b.
2. Was he late? a. b.
3. Is there a phone? a. b.
4. Doesn't she know? a. b.
5. Were they home? a. b.
6. Don't you see? a. b.
7. Can't we stay? a. b.
8. Does it work? a. b.

FIGURE IT OUT

What intonation do you use in yes/no questions? What intonation do you use in negative yes/no questions? Write a rule.

RULE FOR AFFIRMATIVE AND NEGATIVE YES/NO QUESTIONS

Affirmative and negative yes/no questions have *(circle one)*
rising/falling rising intonation.

Now listen to the yes/no questions again and repeat them. The last word in each question has one syllable. Where does the tone rise? Write a rule.

RULE FOR RISING TONES

The tone rises on the ______________ stressed syllable of a yes/no question.

2. READ ALOUD.

DIRECTIONS: Now read the yes/no questions above. Use rising intonation.

3. LISTENING DISCRIMINATION.

DIRECTIONS: Listen to the short yes/no questions. Put a dot over the stressed syllables and words.

EXAMPLE: Was your friend glad?

1. Doesn't he ski?
2. Is it new?
3. Weren't they safe?
4. Can we help?
5. Do classes start soon?
6. Can't you guess?
7. Does the job take time?
8. Isn't it a nice day?

4. READ ALOUD.

DIRECTIONS: Look at the yes/no questions again. Use your Rule for Rising Tones. Figure out which syllable or word rises. Read the yes/no questions aloud.

EXAMPLE: Was your friend glad?

5. LISTENING DISCRIMINATION.

DIRECTIONS: Listen to the yes/no questions. The questions do not have stress on the last syllable.

1. Can she practice?
2. Doesn't it open?
3. Is it a secret?
4. Are you from America?
5. Isn't the test important?
6. Do I need a pencil and paper?
7. Can't you tell me the answer?
8. Were the lessons difficult?

There are some unstressed syllables after the last stress. Rise the tone on the last stress. Continue on the high tone to the end of the yes/no question.

Now listen to the yes/no questions again and repeat them. Practice making the tone rise and keeping it high.

EXAMPLE: Can she practice?

6. READ ALOUD.

DIRECTIONS: Here are some yes/no questions. Some questions have stress on the last syllable. Some questions do *not* have stress on the last syllable. Use your Rule for Rising Tones. Figure out which syllable or word rises.

EXAMPLE: Are you ready to study?

1. Can I ask you a question?
2. Does he remember your number?
3. Is it time for the meeting to start?
4. Do you like to drink coffee for breakfast?
5. Can't we call the office tomorrow?
6. Doesn't the flashlight need batteries?
7. Was his roommate watching the news?
8. Can our instructor help us with math?
9. Aren't you early for your appointment?
10. Does this building have a restroom?

Now read the yes/no questions aloud. Make the tone rise on the correct syllables or words.

7. READ ALOUD. Intonation Contrast.

DIRECTIONS: Yes/no questions have *rising* intonation. *Wh-* questions have *rising/falling* intonation. Practice two kinds of intonation.

EXAMPLE: Are they talking? Why are they talking?

1. Is she coming?	When is she coming?
2. Can't you do it?	Why can't you do it?
3. Do they study?	What time do they study?
4. Are you going?	Where are you going?
5. Was it a long movie?	How long was the movie?
6. Doesn't she want to see it?	Why doesn't she want to see it?
7. Can you help them?	When can you help them?
8. Isn't this your watch?	Where is your watch?
9. Can you drive my friend to the airport?	When can you drive my friend to the airport?
10. Are you going to take a vacation?	Where are you going to take a vacation?

PARTNER 1

8a. SPEAKING. Pair Practice Pictures for Rising Intonation. PARTNER 1. Use this page. PARTNER 2. Turn to page 82.

DIRECTIONS: Here are sixteen boxes. In some boxes, you have pictures. In some boxes, your partner has pictures. You see a list of your partner's pictures. Take turns asking and answering questions about the boxes without pictures. Use rising intonation in your questions.

EXAMPLE:

YOU: Is number three a telephone?

YOUR PARTNER: No, it isn't. Is number one a notebook?

YOU: No, it isn't. Is number three a . . . ?

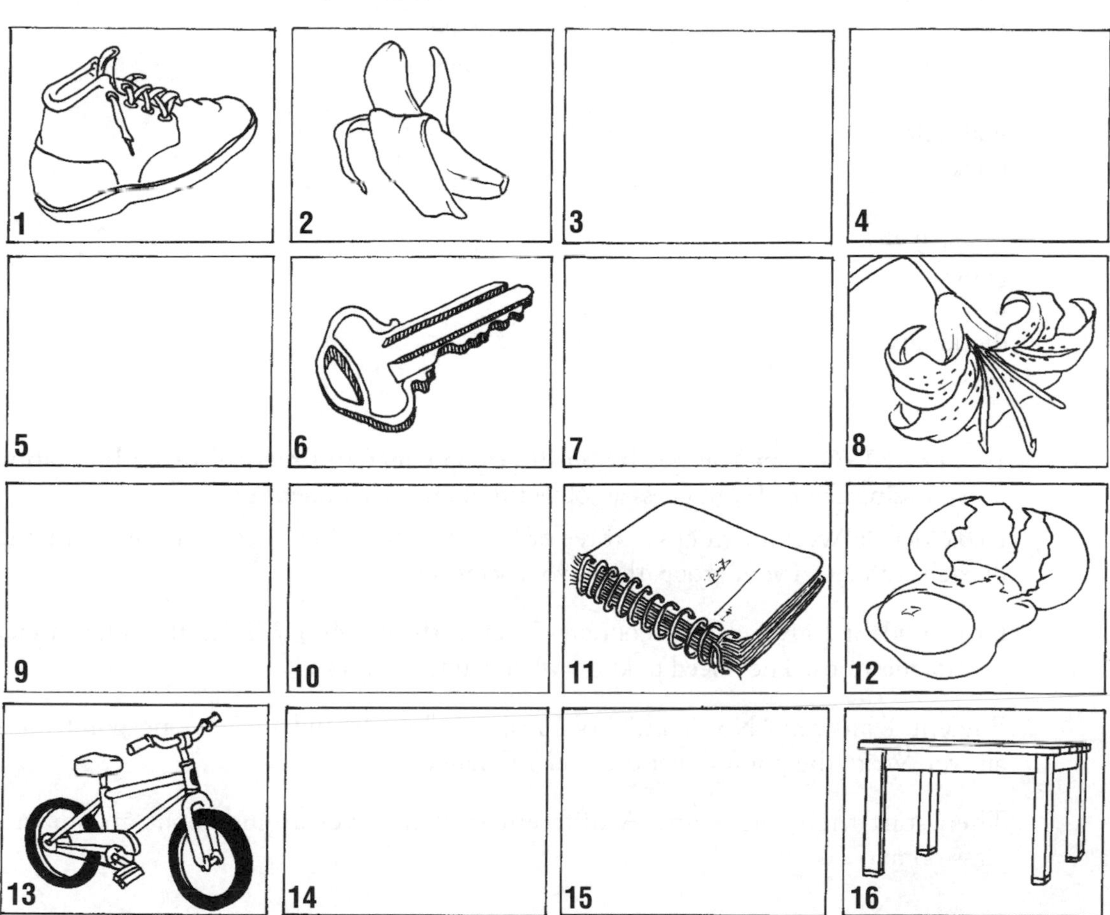

YOUR PARTNER'S PICTURES ARE:

an airplane
an apple
a hammer
a house
a pen
a telephone
a window
a woman

9. SPEAKING. Guided Conversation to Practice Rising Intonation.

DIRECTIONS: Here are a list of *things* and a list of *verbs*. With a partner, take turns asking to borrow things. Use rising intonation in your questions. Use rising/falling intonation in your answers.

EXAMPLE:

STUDENT 1: Is this your ruler?
STUDENT 2: Yes, it is.
STUDENT 1: Can I please use it for a while?
STUDENT 2: Sure. Help yourself.

THINGS	VERBS
notebook	listen to
pen	read
cassette	use
ruler	
umbrella	
book	
radio	
newspaper	
pencil	
map	
dictionary	
eraser	

10. SPEAKING. Can You See It? Small Group Game to Practice Rising Intonation. This is a guessing game. Try to guess an object that another student sees.

DIRECTIONS: Work in groups of three or four students. On a sheet of paper, write the name of each student in your group; this is your score sheet.

First, Student 1 gives a clue about an object in the classroom. Then the other students ask yes/no questions. They need to know what Student 1 sees.

Student 1 answers "No, it isn't" or "Yes, it is." Each student gets one point for a "yes" answer. Write the point under the student's name.

Then start the game again. A different student gives a clue about an object in the classroom.

EXAMPLE:

STUDENT 1: I see something round. Can you see it?
STUDENT 2: Is it the clock?
STUDENT 1: No, it isn't.
STUDENT 3: Is it the light?
STUDENT 1: No, it isn't.
STUDENT 2: Is it the globe?
STUDENT 1: Yes, it is! (Student 2 gets 1 point. Student 2 starts a new game.)
STUDENT 2: I see something black. Can you see it?

Who has the most points in your group? Congratulations!

PARTNER 1

11a. LISTENING DISCRIMINATION AND SPEAKING. Apartment Search. Pair Practice for Rising Intonation and Review of Rising/Falling Intonation. PARTNER 1. Use this page. PARTNER 2. Turn to page 83.

DIRECTIONS: Imagine you are looking for an apartment. Your partner is an apartment manager. You and your partner are on the phone. Use the cues and rising intonation to ask questions.

EXAMPLE: (CUE): . . . two bedrooms?

YOU: I'm calling about your apartment for rent.

Does it have two bedrooms?

MANAGER: No. It has one bedroom.

CUES

. . . a stove?
. . . on the first floor?
. . . an elevator?
. . . in a good neighborhood?
. . . a garage?
. . . a dishwasher?
. . . near shopping?
. . . two bedrooms?
. . . in a safe building?
. . . carpets?

MODEL CONVERSATION

YOU: I'm calling about your apartment for rent. Does it have / Is it ________________ ?
MANAGER: Yes. / No. It ________________ .

Now you are an apartment manager. You have an apartment for rent. You put this ad in the newspaper. Use the ad to answer your partner's questions. Use rising/falling intonation in your answers.

EXAMPLE: YOUR PARTNER: Does it have two bedrooms?

MANAGER: No. It has one bedroom.

> One-bedroom apartment for rent. First floor of a charming older building. Quiet neighborhood 5 miles from schools. Fireplace, balcony, spacious closets, stove, carpets, drapes, garage. $595.00/mo. (914) 555-0011 Ask for manager.

12. INTERVIEW. Pair Practice for Rising Intonation and Review of Rising/Falling Intonation.

DIRECTIONS: Interview a partner about English and Americans. Your partner will interview you, too. Choose who will ask or answer first. Use the cues to ask yes/no questions.

EXAMPLE: (CUE): . . . speak English well?

YOU: Do you speak English well?

You can take notes. Notes help you remember your partner's answers. After the interview, tell the other students in the class about your partner. When you speak to the class about your partner, you need to use rising/falling intonation.

CUES

1. . . . speak English well?
2. . . . understand English easily?
3. . . . have any American friends?
4. . . . watch TV programs in English?
5. . . . read books in English?
6. . . . write letters in English?
7. . . . sometimes dream in English?
8. . . . sometimes think in English?

PARTNER 2

8b. SPEAKING. Pair Practice Pictures for Rising Intonation. PARTNER 2. Use this page.
PARTNER 1. Turn to page 79.

DIRECTIONS: Here are sixteen boxes. In some boxes, you have pictures. In some boxes, your partner has pictures. You see a list of your partner's pictures. Take turns asking and answering questions about boxes with no pictures. Use rising intonation in your questions.

EXAMPLE:

YOU: Is number one a notebook?

YOUR PARTNER: No, it isn't. Is number three a telephone?

YOU: No, it isn't. Is number one a . . . ?

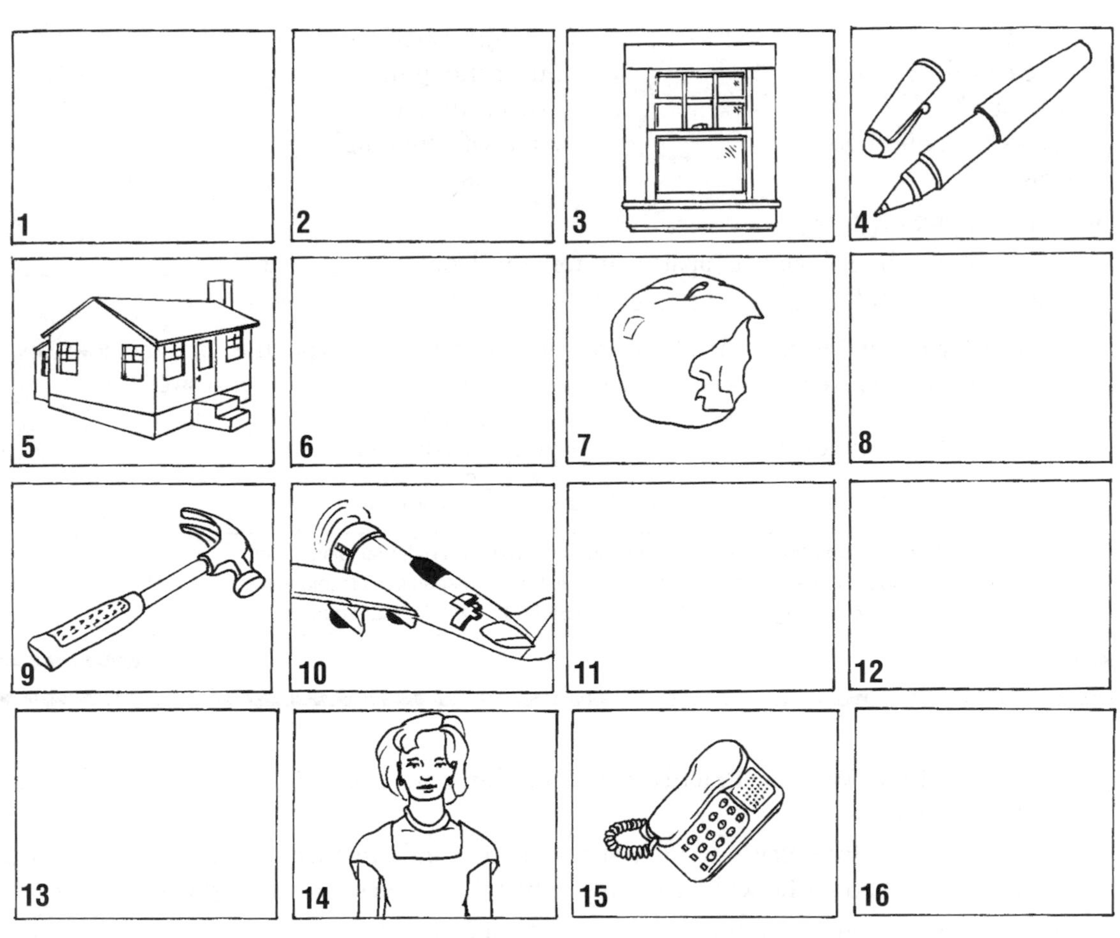

YOUR PARTNER'S PICTURES ARE:

a banana	a key
a bicycle	a notebook
an egg	a shoe
a flower	a table

PAIR PRACTICE: Partner 2

PARTNER 2

11b. LISTENING DISCRIMINATION AND SPEAKING. Apartment Search. Pair Practice for Rising Intonation and Review of Rising/Falling Intonation. PARTNER 2. Use this page. PARTNER 1. Turn to page 81.

DIRECTIONS: You are an apartment manager. You have an apartment for rent. You put this ad in the newspaper. Use the ad to answer your partner's questions. Use rising/falling intonation in your answers.

EXAMPLE:

YOUR PARTNER: Does it have two bedrooms?

MANAGER: No. It has one bedroom.

> One-bedroom apartment for rent. Third floor of a security-gated building. Good quiet neighborhood 3 miles from town. Refrigerator, stove, carpets, drapes, elevator. Parking on street. $650.00/mo. (914) 555-2721 Ask for manager.

Now imagine you are looking for an apartment. Your partner is an apartment manager. You and your partner are on the phone. Use the cues and rising intonation to ask questions.

EXAMPLE: (CUE): . . . two bedrooms?

YOU: I'm calling about your apartment for rent. Does it have two bedrooms?

MANAGER: No. It has one bedroom.

CUES

. . . a pool?
. . . on the top floor?
. . . drapes?
. . . near school?
. . . two bedrooms?
. . . a fireplace?
. . . in a new building?
. . . a closet?
. . . in a quiet neighborhood?
. . . a refrigerator?

MODEL CONVERSATION

YOU: I'm calling about your apartment for rent. Does it have / Is it _______________ ?

MANAGER: Yes. / No. It _______________ .

PAIR PRACTICE: Partner 2

LESSON 9

The Consonants /s/ and /z/; -s *Endings*

PART ONE /s/ and /z/

In English, you find the consonant sound /s/ at the beginning of a word, in the middle of a word, or at the end of a word.

Beginning	*Middle*	*End*
so	passing	yes
send	listen	miss
city	answer	place
seven	bicycle	it's

You find the consonant sound /z/ in the middle of a word or at the end of a word. Not many words have this sound at the beginning.

Beginning	*Middle*	*End*
zone	cousin	does
zoo	reason	nose
zebra	hasn't	is
Xerox	busy	has

Contrasting the Consonants /s/ and /z/

WARM-UP

Look at the pictures. Listen to the words and repeat them.

1. sip /s/

2. zip /z/

ARTICULATION

Look at the pictures. The heads show how to make the sounds.

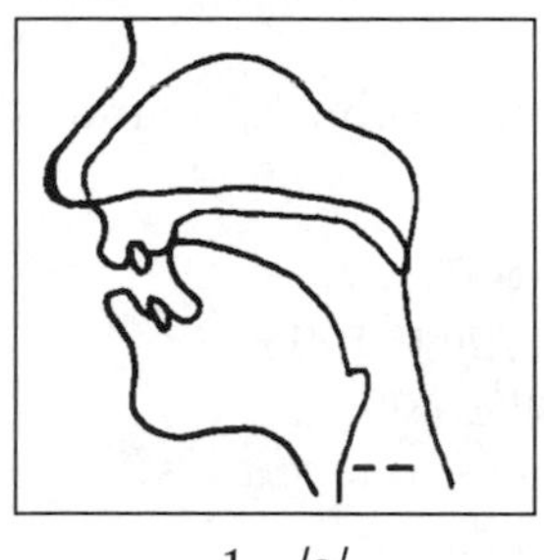

1. /s/

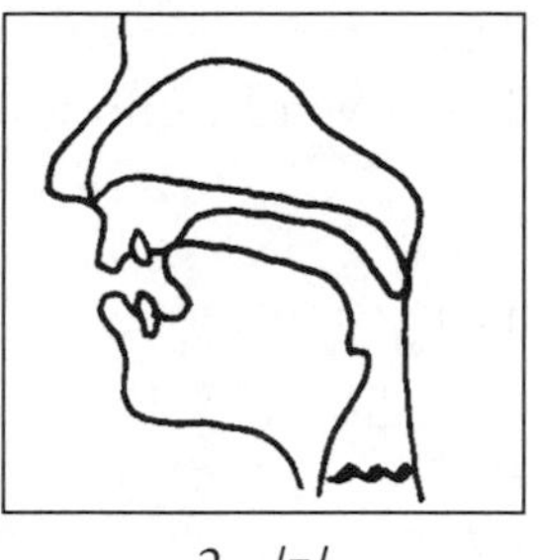

2. /z/

How are the heads the same? How are the heads different?

CONTRAST

Look at the pairs of words. Listen and repeat.

C – Z
ice – eyes

sue – zoo
lacy – lazy

/s/ AND /z/ AT THE END OF A WORD

To clearly contrast /s/ and /z/ at the end of a word, say the vowel before /z/ long. Say the vowel before /s/ short. Listen to this example:

price /s/	pri:ze /z/

Now repeat the pairs of words with /s/ and /z/ at the end. Say the vowel before /z/ long.

/s/	/z/
peace	pea:s
rice	ri:se
lace	lay:s
ice	eye:s
niece	knee:s
place	play:s
loose	lo:se

LISTENING

Many words in English have the contrast between /s/ and /z/. Look again at the *sip* and *zip* pictures on page 84. /s/ is *number 1*. /z/ is *number 2*. Listen to the following words. If you hear /s/ as in *sip*, say "one." If you hear /z/ as in *zip*, say "two."

INTENSIVE PRACTICE

As a class, listen to and repeat the pairs of /s/ and /z/ words you hear.

PRONOUNCE WORDS

Listen to and repeat the /s/ words you hear. Then listen to and repeat the /z/ words you hear.

PRONOUNCE PHRASES

Listen to and repeat the phrases you hear.

PRONOUNCE SENTENCES

Listen to and repeat the sentences you hear.

PRACTICE ACTIVITIES

1. READ ALOUD.

DIRECTIONS: These words, phrases, and sentences have the /s/ sound. Practice reading them aloud.

1. it's, six
   It's six o'clock.
2. yes, see
   Yes, I see it.
3. what's, answer
   What's the answer?
4. it's, sunny
   It's a sunny day.
5. study, this, lesson
   Study this lesson.
6. say, sorry
   Say you're sorry.
7. what's, address
   What's your address?
8. sing, dance
   He can sing and dance.
9. listen, sound
   Listen to the sound.
10. city, yesterday
    We went to the city yesterday.

2. READ ALOUD.

DIRECTIONS: These words, phrases, and sentences have the /z/ sound. Practice reading them aloud.

1. was, busy
   I was very busy.
2. does, music
   Does he like music?
3. where's, magazine
   Where's my magazine?
4. please, close
   Please close the door.
5. use, ours
   You can use ours.
6. he's, Tuesday
   He's leaving next Tuesday.
7. visit, museum
   We'll visit a museum.
8. there's, quiz
   There's a quiz tomorrow.
9. he's, losing
   He's losing the game.
10. has, exam
    She has an exam today.

PARTNER 1

3a. LISTENING DISCRIMINATION AND SPEAKING. Pair Practice Words for /s/ and /z/.

PARTNER 1. Use this page. PARTNER 2. Turn to page 93.

DIRECTIONS: First you are the speaker. Say the words to your partner. You see the consonant sound before each word. For example, you say "Number 1 is *sue*." Repeat any words your partner does not understand.

1. /s/ sue
2. /z/ lies
3. /z/ plays
4. /s/ force
5. /s/ dice
6. /z/ rise
7. /z/ Z
8. /s/ ice
9. /z/ laws
10. /z/ bays

Now you are the listener. Your partner will say some words. Circle the words you hear. Ask your partner to repeat any words you do not understand. Number 11 is an example.

11.	price	(prize)
12.	lacy	lazy
13.	peace	peas
14.	hiss	his
15.	niece	knees
16.	pace	pays
17.	bus	buzz
18.	loose	lose
19.	sip	zip
20.	racing	raising

Now compare answers with your partner.

PARTNER 1

4a. LISTENING DISCRIMINATION AND SPEAKING. Pair Practice Sentences for /s/ and /z/. PARTNER 1. Use this page. PARTNER 2. Turn to page 93.

DIRECTIONS: First you are the speaker. Say the sentences to your partner. You see the consonant sound before each sentence. Repeat any sentences your partner does not understand.

1. /z/ Did you see the PLAYS?
2. /s/ This man will give you the PRICE.
3. /s/ The LOSS made him angry.
4. /z/ Don is asking about a RAISE.
5. /z/ The light is shining on my EYES.

Now you are the listener. Your partner will say some sentences. Circle the word you hear. Ask your partner to repeat any sentences you do not understand. Number 6 is an example.

6. Give him some ____________ .
   a. peace b. (peas)
7. I'm ____________ it.
   a. sipping b. zipping
8. Your wallet is near my ____________ .
   a. niecc b. knees
9. This is a picture of a ____________ .
   a. racer b. razor
10. Our boat is near the ____________ .
    a. base b. bays

Now compare answers with your partner.

PART TWO Pronunciation of -s Endings

The pronunciation of the *-s* ending in English is important. English speakers use it very often. The example sentences show different meanings of *-s* in English grammar.

EXAMPLES:

They own three cars. (plural noun)

The baby's coat is too small. (possessive)

Sally usually gets up at 6:30. (third person singular)

He's waiting for the bus. (contraction of *is*)

The *-s* ending in English can sound like /z/, /s/, or like a separate syllable /ɪz/. The pronunciation of *-s* is regular. Listen to the *-s* endings of the words in the columns on page 88. Mark each column with /z/, /s/, or /ɪz/. All words in each column have the same sound for *-s*.

/ /		/ /		/ /	
word ends in:		word ends in:		word ends in:	
sound	***word***	***sound***	***word***	***sound***	***word***
/p/	stops	/b/	robs	/s/	misses
	hopes		clubs		dresses
	sleeps	/d/	reads		buses
/t/	it's		finds	/z/	noises
	hats	/g/	dogs		loses
	writes		eggs		prizes
/k/	books	/v/	lives	/ʃ/	washes
	speaks		selves		brushes
	Rick's	/ð/	breathes		pushes
/f/	laughs	/m/	comes	/tʃ/	watches
	Jeff's		Tim's		catches
	roofs	/n/	runs		matches
/θ/	paths		gardens	/dʒ/	changes
	Beth's	/ŋ/	brings		edges
	earth's		things		messages
		/l/	bills		
			travels		
		/r/	cars		
			answers		
		vowel	goes		
			she's		
			shows		

FIGURE IT OUT

Look at pages viii–ix in "To the Student." It will help you figure out the rules.

The words in the first column end in /p/, /t/, /k/, /f/, or /θ/. How are these sounds similar? How is /s/ similar to these sounds? Write a rule.

RULE

Start with a word that ends in the consonant sound /p/, /t/, /k/, /f/, or /θ/.
The vocal cords are *(circle one)* moving not moving for these consonant sounds. Add *-s* and pronounce *-s* / /.

The words in the second column end in /b/, /d/, /g/, /v/, /ð/, /m/, /n/, /ŋ/, /l/, /r/, or a vowel. How are these sounds similar? How is /z/ similar to these sounds? Write a rule.

RULE

Start with a word that ends in the consonant sound /b/, /d/, /g/, /v/, /ð/, /m/, /n/, /ŋ/, /l/, /r/, or any vowel.
The vocal cords are *(circle one)* moving not moving for these consonants and all vowel sounds. Add *-s* and pronounce *-s* / /.

The words in the last column end in /s/, /z/, /ʃ/, /tʃ/, and /dʒ/. They are all noisy sounds. Try to pronounce the words in the third column with /s/ or /z/ for *-s* endings. Now pronounce the words in the third column with /ɪz/ for *-s* endings. Which of the three sounds is easiest to hear? Write a rule.

RULE

Start with a word that ends in the consonant sound /s/, /z/, /ʃ/, /tʃ/, or /dʒ/. These five sounds are ________________. Add *-s* and pronounce *-s* /   /.

PRONOUNCE -S ENDINGS.

Listen to and repeat the words on page 88. Then say them on your own. Read going across, one word from each column. Pronounce the *-s* correctly.

EXAMPLE:

stops	robs	misses
/s/	/z/	/ɪz/

PRACTICE ACTIVITIES

1. **SPEAKING. Pair or Group Practice for Plural *-s* Endings.** Here is a picture of boxes. Each box has more than one object in it.

DIRECTIONS: Take turns asking and answering questions about the boxes. You and your group need to pronounce the *-s* endings.

EXAMPLE:

STUDENT 1: What's in box number two?
STUDENT 2: Eleven rings. What's in box number five?
STUDENT 3: Nine peaches. What's . . .

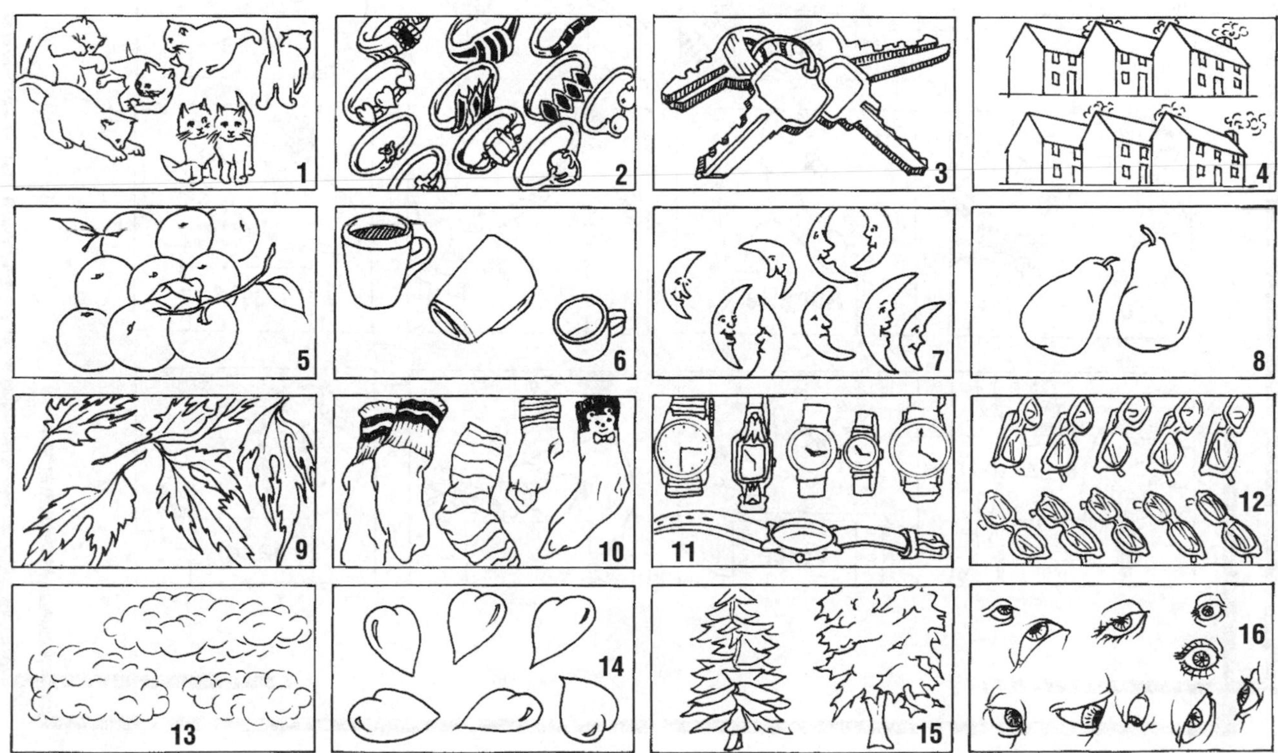

PARTNER 1

2a. SPEAKING AND LISTENING. Pair Practice Pictures for Contractions of *is* and Possessive. PARTNER 1. Use this page. PARTNER 2. Turn to page 94.

DIRECTIONS: Ask your partner about the pictures. Find out the names of people with *no names*. Write their names below the pictures.

Your partner will ask you about the pictures, too. Answer about the pictures *with names*. You and your partner need to pronounce the *-s* for the contraction of *is* and the possessive *'s*.

EXAMPLE:

PARTNER 2: Who<u>'s</u> sewing?
PARTNER 1: Mabel<u>'s</u> sewing.
PARTNER 2: How do you spell Mabel<u>'s</u> name?
PARTNER 1: M-A-B-E-L. Who<u>'s</u> riding a bicycle?
PARTNER 2: Jack<u>'s</u> riding a bicycle.

3. SPEAKING. Guided Conversation to Practice Plural and Possessive.

DIRECTIONS: Imagine that you are going shopping. Here is a shopping list. Here is a list of stores. Take turns asking and answering questions. You and your partner need to pronounce the *-s* of plural nouns and possessive *'s* correctly.

EXAMPLE:

FRIEND: What do you want to get at Andy's Flower Shop?
SHOPPER: I'll get some flower pots.
FRIEND: Where are you going to buy the matches?
SHOPPER: I'm going to buy them at Jess's Grocery Store.
FRIEND: How many potato chips do you want to get?
SHOPPER: I think I'll get two bags of potato chips.

SHOPPING LIST
strawberries
cakes
paper cups
oranges
matches
apple pies
flower pots
bottles of juice
candy bars
potato chips
roses
loaves of bread
cans of Coke
hot dogs

STORES
Smith's Bakery
Jess's Grocery Store
Andy's Flower Shop
Mitch's Supermarket

MODEL CONVERSATION

FRIEND: What do you want to get at ____________________?
SHOPPER: I'll get some ____________________.
FRIEND: Where are you going to buy the____________________?
SHOPPER: I'm going to buy them at ____________________.
FRIEND: How many ____________________ do you want to get?
SHOPPER: I think I'll get ____________________.

4. LISTENING DISCRIMINATION AND SPEAKING. Pair or Group Review of /s/ and /z/ and *-s* Endings of Third Person Singular Verbs. Here is a chart of people and some things they do every week. The check marks (✓) tell you how often each person does each thing.

DIRECTIONS: Take turns asking and answering questions about the people. Use *always*, *sometimes*, or *seldom* in your answer.

EXAMPLE:

STUDENT 1: Does Cindy read magazines?
/z//s/ /z/ /z/
STUDENT 2: Cindy sometimes reads magazines. Does Charles take walks?
/s/ /s/ /z/ /z/ /z/ /z/ /z/ /z/ /s/
STUDENT 3: Charles seldom takes walks. Does Isaac watch TV?
/z//s/ /s/ /s/ /z/ /z/

✔✔✔ = always ✔✔ = sometimes ✔ = seldom

	Bessie	Isaac	Susan	Cindy	Charles
Watch TV	✔✔✔	✔✔✔	✔	✔	✔✔
Write letters	✔✔✔	✔	✔✔✔	✔	✔✔
Read magazines	✔	✔✔✔	✔✔	✔✔	✔✔✔
Study	✔	✔	✔✔	✔✔	✔
Make phone calls	✔✔	✔	✔	✔✔	✔
Take walks	✔✔✔	✔✔	✔	✔✔✔	✔
Read books	✔	✔	✔✔	✔✔	✔✔✔

5. INTERVIEW. Pair Practice for *-s* Endings of Third Person Singular Verbs.

DIRECTIONS: Interview a partner. Use the ten cues to ask questions. You can take notes to remember your partner's answers.

EXAMPLE: (CUE): . . . have breakfast?
YOU: What time / When do you usually have breakfast?

Your partner will interview you, too. Choose who will ask or answer first. After the interviews, tell the other students in the class about your partner. You can use your notes. When you speak to the class about your partner, use *she* or *he*. Pronounce the *-s* endings of the verbs.

CUES

1. . . . get up?
2. . . . go to school/work?
3. . . . take a break?
4. . . . eat lunch?
5. . . . get home?
6. . . . eat dinner?
7. . . . wash the dishes?
8. . . . go to bed?

PARTNER 2

3b. LISTENING DISCRIMINATION AND SPEAKING. Pair Practice Words for /s/ and /z/.
PARTNER 2. Use this page. PARTNER 1. Turn to page 86.

DIRECTIONS: First you are the listener. Your partner will say some words. Circle the words you hear. Ask your partner to repeat any words you do not understand. Number 1 is an example.

1. (sue) zoo
2. lice lies
3. place plays
4. force fours
5. dice dies
6. rice rise
7. C Z
8. ice eyes
9. loss laws
10. base bays

Now you are the speaker. Say the words to your partner. You see the consonant sound before each word. For example, you say "Number 11 is *prize*." Repeat any words your partner does not understand.

11. /z/ prize
12. /z/ lazy
13. /s/ peace
14. /s/ hiss
15. /z/ knees (Do not pronounce *k*. It is silent.)
16. /s/ pace
17. /z/ buzz
18. /s/ loose
19. /s/ sip
20. /z/ raising

Now compare answers with your partner.

PARTNER 2

4b. LISTENING DISCRIMINATION AND SPEAKING. Pair Practice Sentences for /s/ and /z/. PARTNER 2. Use this page. PARTNER 1. Turn to page 87.

DIRECTIONS: First you are the listener. Your partner will say some sentences. Circle the word you hear. Ask your partner to repeat any sentences you do not understand. Number 1 is an example.

1. Did you see the ____________ ?
   a. place b. (plays)
2. This man will give you the ____________ .
   a. price b. prize
3. The ____________ made him angry.
   a. loss b. laws
4. Don is asking about a ____________ .
   a. race b. raise
5. The light is shining on my ____________ .
   a. ice b. eyes

Now you are the speaker. Say the sentences to your partner. You see the consonant sound before each sentence. Repeat any sentences your partner does not understand.

6. /z/ Give him some PEAS.
7. /z/ I'm ZIPPING it.
8. /z/ Your wallet is near my KNEES.
9. /s/ This is a picture of a RACER.
10. /z/ Our boat is near the BAYS.

Now compare answers with your partner.

PAIR PRACTICE: Partner 2

PARTNER 2

2b. SPEAKING AND LISTENING. Pair Practice Pictures for Contractions of *is* and Possessive. PARTNER 2. Use this page. PARTNER 1. Turn to page 90.

DIRECTIONS: Ask your partner about the pictures. Find out the names of people with *no names*. Write their names below the pictures.

Your partner will ask you about the pictures, too. Answer about the pictures *with names*. You and your partner need to pronounce the *-s* for the contraction of *is* and the possessive *'s*.

EXAMPLE:

PARTNER 2: Who<u>'s</u> sewing?
PARTNER 1: Mabel<u>'s</u> sewing.
PARTNER 2: How do you spell Mabel<u>'s</u> name?
PARTNER 1: M-A-B-E-L. Who<u>'s</u> riding a bicycle?
PARTNER 2: Jack<u>'s</u> riding a bicycle.

The Consonants /t/ and /d/; -ed Endings

LESSON 10

PART ONE /t/ and /d/

In English, you can find the consonant sound /t/ at the beginning of a word, in the middle of a word, or at the end of a word.

Beginning	*Middle*	*End*
two	empty	wait
ten	doctor	write
tall	mistake	what
take	until	forget

You can find the consonant sound /d/ at the beginning of a word, in the middle of a word, or at the end of a word, too.

Beginning	*Middle*	*End*
do	under	sad
day	study	find
down	radio	need
desk	address	loud

Contrasting the Consonants /t/ and /d/

WARM-UP

Look at the pictures. Listen to the words and repeat them.

1. time /t/

2. dime /d/

ARTICULATION

Look at the pictures. The heads show how to make the sounds.

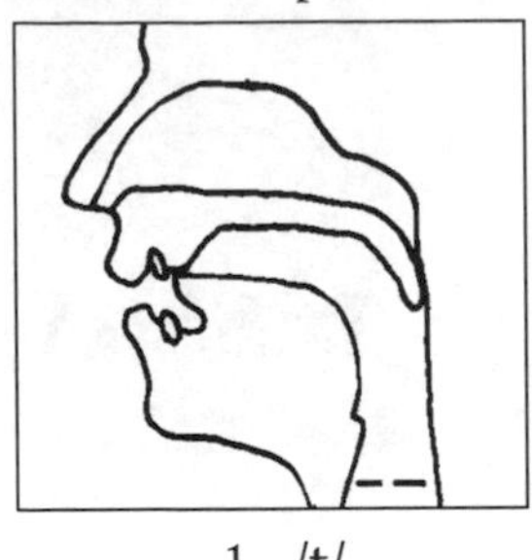

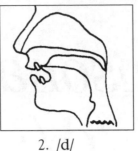

1. /t/

2. /d/

How are the heads the same? How are the heads different?

CONTRAST

Look at the pairs of words. Listen and repeat.

tie – die   ton – done   T – D   town – down

/t/ AT THE BEGINNING OF A WORD

To clearly pronounce /t/ at the beginning of a word, push the air from your mouth. Put your hand in front of your mouth. Say /t/. You can feel the air.

Listen to this example: ten, ten, ten

Now repeat the words with /t/ at the beginning. Push the air from your mouth when you say /t/.

took	tie	tip
toy	teach	table

/t/ LIKE /d/ IN THE MIDDLE OF A WORD

Sometimes, /t/ sounds like a very fast /d/. You find this special /t/ between two vowel sounds. This /t/ is never at the beginning of a stressed syllable. Listen to these examples:

water	eating	city
notice	united	beautiful

/t/ does not sound like /d/ when a consonant sound is right before /t/ or right after /t/. Listen to these examples:

country	interest	chemistry
acting	sometimes	electric

LISTENING

Many words in English have the contrast between /t/ and /d/. Look again at the *time* and *dime* pictures on page 95. /t/ is *number 1*. /d/ is *number 2*. Listen to the following words. If you hear /t/ as in *time*, say "one." If you hear /d/ as in *dime*, say "two."

INTENSIVE PRACTICE

As a class, listen to and repeat the pairs of /t/ and /d/ words you hear.

PRONOUNCE WORDS

Listen to and repeat the /t/ words you hear. Then listen to and repeat the /d/ words you hear.

PRONOUNCE PHRASES

Listen to and repeat the phrases you hear.

PRONOUNCE SENTENCES

Listen to and repeat the sentences you hear.

PRACTICE ACTIVITIES

PARTNER 1

1a. LISTENING DISCRIMINATION AND SPEAKING. Pair Practice Words for /t/ and /d/.
PARTNER 1. Use this page. PARTNER 2. Turn to page 103.

DIRECTIONS: First you are the speaker. Say the words to your partner. You see the consonant sound before each word. For example, you say "Number 1 is *tan*." Repeat any words your partner does not understand.

1. /t/	tan	5. /t/	tie
2. /d/	doe	6. /d/	D
3. /d/	down	7. /d/	do
4. /t/	tense	8. /t/	ton

Now you are the listener. Your partner will say some words. Circle the words you hear. Ask your partner to repeat any words you do not understand. Number 9 is an example.

9.	tent	(dent)	13	try	dry
10.	tip	dip	14.	tile	dial
11.	tore	door	15.	two	do
12.	time	dime	16.	town	down

Now compare answers with your partner.

PARTNER 1

2a. LISTENING DISCRIMINATION AND SPEAKING. Pair Practice Sentences for /t/ and /d/.
PARTNER 1. Use this page. PARTNER 2. Turn to page 103.

DIRECTIONS: First you are the speaker. Say the sentences to your partner. You see the consonant sound before each sentence. Repeat any sentences your partner does not understand.

1. /t/ I don't have the TIME.
2. /d/ It was DENSE.
3. /d/ Don't DRIP on the rug.
4. /t/ He spells his name with a T.

Now you are the listener. Your partner will say some sentences. Circle the word you hear. Ask your partner to repeat any sentences you do not understand. Number 5 is an example.

5. Put this ____________ on the map.
   a. (town) b. down
6. I don't see the ____________ .
   a. tent b. dent
7. How do you spell "____________" ?
   a. true b. drew
8. You need a ____________ to fix it.
   a. tile b. dial

Now compare answers with your partner.

PARTNER 1

3a. LISTENING DISCRIMINATION AND SPEAKING. Pair Practice for /t/ and /d/.
PARTNER 1. Use this page. PARTNER 2. Turn to page 104.

DIRECTIONS: Ask your partner questions about the clothes in the picture below. Find out the prices of clothes with *no prices*. Write the prices on the tags.

Your partner will ask you about the clothes, too. Answer about the clothes *with prices*. You and your partner need to pronounce the /t/ and /d/ at the beginning, middle, and end of words.

EXAMPLE:

PARTNER 2: How much is the shirt?
PARTNER 1: It's ten dollars and twenty-five cents. How much are the boots?
PARTNER 2: They're fifty-two dollars. How much . . .

PART TWO Pronunciation of *-ed* Endings

The pronunciation of the *-ed* ending in English is important. English speakers use it very often. The example sentences show different meanings of *-ed* in English grammar.

EXAMPLES:

They watched a movie. (simple past tense)
A locked door isn't easy to open. (adjective formed from a verb)

The *-ed* ending in English can sound like /d/, /t/, or like a separate syllable /ɪd/. The pronunciation of *-ed* is regular.

Listen to the *-ed* endings of the words in the columns below. Mark each column with /d/, /t/, or /ɪd/. All words in each column have the same sound for *-ed.*

/ /
word ends in:

sound	***word***
/p/	stopped
	kidnapped
	helped
/k/	talked
	worked
	looked
/f/	laughed
	knifed
	golfed
/s/	missed
	danced
	passed
/tʃ/	watched
	matched
	reached
/ʃ/	wished
	washed
	cashed

/ /
word ends in:

sound	***word***
/b/	robbed
	described
/g/	jogged
	begged
/v/	lived
	moved
/ð/	breathed
/z/	used
	closed
/dʒ/	changed
	managed
/m/	dreamed
	armed
/n/	learned
	listened
/ŋ/	hanged
	wronged
/l/	called
	traveled
/r/	bored
	answered
vowel	played
	followed

/ /
word ends in:

sound	***word***
/t/	lasted
	wanted
	visited
	corrected
/d/	needed
	ended
	added
	crowded

FIGURE IT OUT

Look at pages viii–ix in "To the Student." It will help you figure out the rules.

The words in the first column end in /p/, /k/, /f/, /s/, /tʃ/, or /ʃ/. How are these sounds similar? How is /t/ similar to these sounds? Write a rule.

RULE

Start with a word that ends in the consonant sound /p/, /k/, /f/, /s/, /tʃ/, or /ʃ/.
The vocal cords are *(circle one)* moving not moving for these consonant sounds. Add *-ed* and pronounce *-ed* / /.

The words in the second column end in /b/, /g/, /v/, /ð/, /z/, /dʒ/, /m/, /n/, /ŋ/, /l/, /r/, or a vowel. How are these sounds similar? How is /d/ similar to these sounds? Write a rule.

RULE

Start with a word that ends in the consonant sound /b/, /g/, /v/, /ð/, /z/, /dʒ/, /m/, /n/, /ŋ/, /l/, /r/, or any vowel.

The vocal cords are *(circle one)* moving not moving for these consonants and all vowel sounds. Add *-ed* and pronounce *-ed* / /.

The words in the last column end in /t/ and /d/. Try to pronounce the words in the third column with /t/ or /d/ for *-ed* endings. Now pronounce the words in the third column with /ɪd/ for *-ed* endings. Which of the three sounds is easiest to pronounce? Write a rule.

RULE

Start with a word that ends in the consonant sound /t/ or /d/.

These two sounds are *(circle one)* the same as different from the regular sounds for *-ed* endings. Add *-ed* and pronounce *-ed* / /.

PRONOUNCE *-ED* ENDINGS.

Listen to and repeat the words in the columns on page 99. Then say them on your own. Read going across, one word from each column. Pronounce the *-ed* correctly.

EXAMPLE:

stopped	robbed	lasted
/t/	/d/	/ɪd/

PRACTICE ACTIVITIES

1. READ ALOUD AND CHANGE. Pair or Group Practice for *-ed* Endings. Here are three short stories. They are in the simple present tense.

DIRECTIONS: Take turns with other people in your group. One student reads a story in the present tense. Then another student reads the same story but changes the verbs to past tense. You and the other people in your group need to pronounce *-ed.*

EXAMPLE (STORY 1):

STUDENT 1: Every day, Ken gets up at 6:30. He hurries to the bathroom, . . . What did Ken do yesterday?

STUDENT 2: Yesterday, Ken got up at 6:30. He hurried to the bathroom, . . .

STORY 1. Every day, Ken gets up at 6:30. He hurries to the bathroom and washes and dries his face. He brushes his teeth, combs his hair, and dresses. Then he walks to the kitchen and pours himself some coffee. After that, he kisses his wife good-bye. He takes his car to work and arrives at 8:00. What did Ken do yesterday?

Yesterday . . .

STORY 2. Janet works as a secretary for Mr. Benson. She answers the phone, and sometimes she places long-distance calls for her boss. She often types letters and files papers. She opens Mr. Benson's mail every morning at 10:00. She helps Mr. Benson's receptionist at lunch time and locks the office at 5:00. What did Janet do last year?

Last year, . . .

<u>STORY 3</u>. Mr. and Mrs. Stuart take the same vacation every summer. They arrive at their beach house in August. They unpack their car and then visit the beach. Sometimes they carry their lunch to the beach for a picnic. They suntan and sail. Sometimes they play tennis. In the evening, they fix dinner at their beach house. At the end of August, they clean the house. Then they pack the car and travel back to the city. What did they do last summer?

Last summer, . . .

2. STUDY AND READ ALOUD. Here is a list of thirty regular past tense verbs.

DIRECTIONS: Put each verb in one of the columns. Number 1 is an example. Then read aloud each verb in each column. Pronounce /t/, /d/, and /ɪd/ correctly as you read aloud.

1. looked ✔
2. pronounced
3. tasted
4. missed
5. excused
6. added
7. lived
8. studied
9. interested
10. rushed
11. dialed
12. judged
13. attached
14. carried
15. enjoyed
16. cleared
17. excited
18. showed
19. poured
20. cried
21. mixed
22. spelled
23. stepped
24. acted
25. happened
26. wished
27. practiced
28. shaved
29. named
30. agreed

***-ed* sounds like /t/**	***-ed* sounds like /d/**	***-ed* sounds like /ɪd/**
looked		

PARTNER 1

3a. LISTENING DISCRIMINATION AND SPEAKING. **Challenge! Pair Practice for *-ed* Endings. PARTNER 1. Use this page. PARTNER 2. Turn to page 105.

DIRECTIONS: Say these sentences to your partner. Then listen to your partner's response. If your partner does not make a logical response, repeat the sentence.

EXAMPLES:

YOU:	They didn't miss the bus.
YOUR PARTNER:	You're right. They hurried.
YOU:	He talked very loudly.
YOUR PARTNER:	You're right. He shouted.

1. The street is wet.
2. They didn't work.
3. It's dark in here.
4. She didn't go home.
5. Tom doesn't live here anymore.
6. The TV works.

Now listen to your partner's sentences. Then make a logical response from the list. Your partner will repeat the sentence if your response is not logical. Pronounce the *-ed* endings.

RESPONSES

You're right. It's locked.
You're right. He's married.
You're right. She smiled.
You're right. It stopped.
You're right. They studied.
You're right. It's washed.

4. INTERVIEW. Pair Practice for *-ed* Endings of Simple Past Regular Verbs.

DIRECTIONS: Interview a partner. Use the seven cues to ask questions. You can take notes to remember your partner's answers.

EXAMPLE:

(CUE):	. . . yesterday?
YOU:	What did you do yesterday?

Your partner will interview you, too. Choose who will ask or answer first. After the interviews, tell the other students in the class about your partner. You can use your notes. When you speak to the class about your partner, you need to pronounce the *-ed* endings on the verbs.

CUES

1. . . . as soon as you got up today?
2. . . . yesterday?
3. . . . the day before yesterday?
4. . . . right before class?
5. . . . last Monday?
6. . . . last weekend?
7. . . . during your last vacation?

PARTNER 2

1b. LISTENING DISCRIMINATION AND SPEAKING. Pair Practice Words for /t/ and /d/.
PARTNER 2. Use this page. PARTNER 1. Turn to page 97.

DIRECTIONS: First you are the listener. Your partner will say some words. Circle the words you hear. Ask your partner to repeat any words you do not understand. Number 1 is an example.

1. (tan) Dan
2. toe doe
3. town down
4. tense dense
5. tie die
6. T D
7. two do
8. ton done

Now you are the speaker. Say the words to your partner. You see the consonant sound before each word. For example, you say "Number 9 is *dent*." Repeat any words your partner does not understand.

9. /d/ dent
10. /d/ dip
11. /t/ tore
12. /d/ dime
13. /t/ try
14. /t/ tile
15. /d/ do
16. /d/ down

Now compare answers with your partner.

PARTNER 2

2b. LISTENING DISCRIMINATION AND SPEAKING. Pair Practice Sentences for /t/ and /d/.
PARTNER 2. Use this page. PARTNER 1. Turn to page 97.

DIRECTIONS: First you are the listener. Your partner will say some sentences. Circle the word you hear. Ask your partner to repeat any sentences you do not understand. Number 1 is an example.

1. I don't have the ____________ .
   a. (time) b. dime
2. It was ____________ .
   a. tense b. dense
3. Don't ____________ on the rug.
   a. trip b. drip
4. He spells his name with a ____________ .
   a. T b. D

Now you are the speaker. Say the sentences to your partner. You see the consonant sound before each sentence. Repeat any sentences your partner does not understand.

5. /t/ Put this TOWN on the map.
6. /d/ I don't see the DENT.
7. /d/ How do you spell "DREW"?
8. /t/ You need a TILE to fix it.

Now compare answers with your partner.

PARTNER 2

3b. LISTENING DISCRIMINATION AND SPEAKING. Pair Practice for /t/ and /d/.
PARTNER 2. Use this page. PARTNER 1. Turn to page 98.

DIRECTIONS: Ask your partner questions about the clothes in the picture. Find out the prices of clothes with *no prices*. Write the prices on the tags.

Your partner will ask you about the clothes, too. Answer about the clothes *with prices*. You and your partner need to pronounce the /t/ and /d/ at the beginning, middle, and end of words.

EXAMPLE:

PARTNER 2: How much is the shirt?
PARTNER 1: It's ten dollars and twenty-five cents. How much are the boots?
PARTNER 2: They're fifty-two dollars. How much . . .

PARTNER 2

3b. LISTENING DISCRIMINATION AND SPEAKING. **Challenge! Pair Practice for *-ed* Endings. PARTNER 2. Use this page. PARTNER 1. Turn to page 102.

DIRECTIONS: Listen to your partner's sentences. Then make a logical response from the list. Your partner will repeat the sentence if your response is not logical. Pronounce the *-ed* endings.

EXAMPLES:

YOUR PARTNER: They didn't miss the bus.
YOU: You're right. They hurried.
YOUR PARTNER: He talked very loudly.
YOU: You're right. He shouted.

RESPONSES

You're right. The curtains are closed.
You're right. It's fixed.
You're right. He moved.
You're right. They played.
You're right. It rained.
You're right. She stayed here.

Now say these sentences to your partner. Then listen to your partner's response. If your partner does not make a logical response, repeat the sentence.

7. My shirt is clean.
8. She's happy.
9. The bus isn't moving.
10. I can't open the door.
11. They passed the test.
12. He's not single.

LESSON 11

The Consonants /θ/ and /ð/

PART ONE /θ/ and /t/

In English, you find the consonant sound /θ/ (as in the word *th*ink) at the beginning of a word, in the middle of a word, or at the end of a word.

Beginning	*Middle*	*End*
thing	anything	month
third	something	with
three	birthday	both
thanks	southwest	math

In Lesson 10, you learned about the sound /t/ at the beginning of a word, in the middle of a word, or at the end of a word.

Contrasting the Consonants /θ/ and /t/

WARM-UP

Look at the pictures. Listen to the words and repeat them.

1. three /θ/

2. tree /t/

ARTICULATION

Look at the pictures. The heads show how to make the sounds.

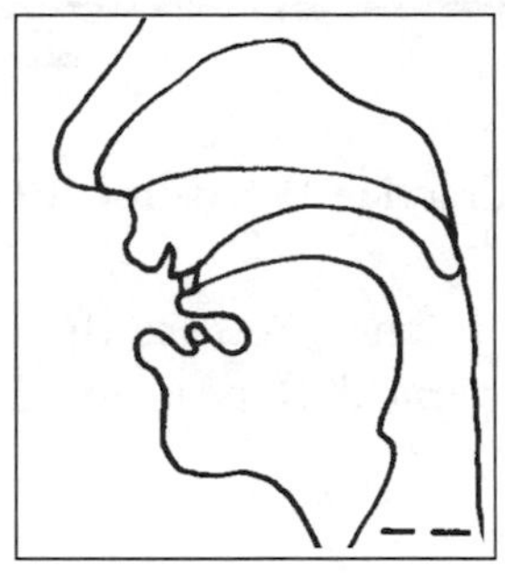

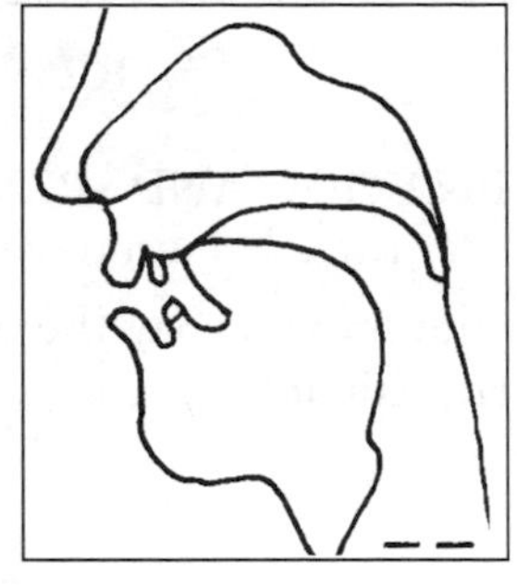

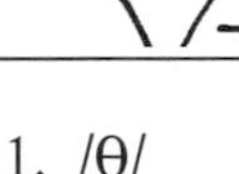

1. /θ/ 2. /t/

How are the heads the same? How are the heads different?

CONTRAST

Look at the pairs of words. Listen and repeat.

thin – tin

thought – taught

path – pat

both – boat

/t/ AT THE BEGINNING OF A WORD AND AT THE END OF A WORD

Turn to page 95, Lesson 10. Review the sound of /t/ at the beginning and end of words.

LISTENING

Many words in English have the contrast between /θ/ and /t/. Look again at the *three* and *tree* pictures on page 106. /θ/ is *number 1*. /t/ is *number 2*. Listen to the following words. If you hear /θ/ as in *three*, say "one." If you hear /t/ as in *tree*, say "two."

INTENSIVE PRACTICE

As a class, listen to and repeat the pairs of /θ/ and /t/ words you hear.

PRONOUNCE WORDS

Listen to and repeat the /θ/ words you hear. Then listen to and repeat the /t/ words you hear.

PRONOUNCE PHRASES

Listen to and repeat the phrases you hear.

PRONOUNCE SENTENCES

Listen to and repeat the sentences you hear.

PARTNER 1

1a. LISTENING DISCRIMINATION AND SPEAKING. Pair Practice Words for /θ/ and /t/.
PARTNER 1. Use this page. PARTNER 2. Turn to page 119.

DIRECTIONS: First you are the speaker. Say the words to your partner. You see the consonant sound before each word. For example, you say "Number 1 is *theme*." Repeat any words your partner does not understand.

1. /θ/ theme
2. /t/ tie
3. /t/ mat
4. /θ/ threw
5. /θ/ both
6. /θ/ thin
7. /t/ taught
8. /θ/ tenth
9. /t/ boot
10. /t/ tree

Now you are the listener. Your partner will say some words. Circle the words you hear. Ask your partner to repeat any words you do not understand. Number 11 is an example.

11. (tenth) tent
12. booth boot
13. thought taught
14. math mat
15. three tree
16. thank tank
17. threw true
18. both boat
19. thigh tie
20. thin tin

Now compare answers with your partner.

PARTNER 1

2a. LISTENING DISCRIMINATION AND SPEAKING. Pair Practice Sentences for /θ/ and /t/.
PARTNER 1. Use this page. PARTNER 2. Turn to page 119.

DIRECTIONS: First you are the speaker. Say the sentences to your partner. You see the consonant sound before each sentence. Repeat any sentences your partner does not understand.

1. /t/ Bob spilled coffee on his TIE.
2. /θ/ Which one is your THEME?
3. /θ/ They want money for THANKS.
4. /t/ Is it TRUE?

Now you are the listener. Your partner will say some sentences. Circle the word you hear. Ask your partner to repeat any sentences you do not understand. Number 5 is an example.

5. I'll use a ________________ pan.
   a. (thin) b. tin
6. This is no place for a ______________ .
   a. bath b. bat
7. Joe ________________ for many years.
   a. thought b. taught
8. You can't fit in this ________________ .
   a. booth b. boot

Now compare answers with your partner.

PARTNER 1

3a. SPEAKING AND LISTENING. Pair Practice for /θ/ and /t/. PARTNER 1. Use this page. PARTNER 2. Turn to page 120.

DIRECTIONS: You want to buy a ticket for tomorrow's performance at the Little Theater. You want to sit near one of your friends on the list. Ask your partner where your friends are going to sit. Pronounce /θ/ and /t/ correctly.

EXAMPLE:

YOU: Where's Thelma going to sit?
YOUR PARTNER: Thelma's going to sit in the third row in the fourth seat.

FRIENDS

Thelma	Seth	Timothy
Travis	Patricia	Ruth
Tammy	Judith	Elizabeth

Now here is the Little Theater. Your partner wants to buy a ticket for next week. Your partner will ask you where his or her friends are going to sit. Tell your partner what *row* and *seat* each person is going to sit in. Pronounce /θ/ and /t/ correctly.

EXAMPLE:

YOUR PARTNER: Where's Anthony going to sit?
YOU: Anthony is going to sit in the fifth row in the third seat.

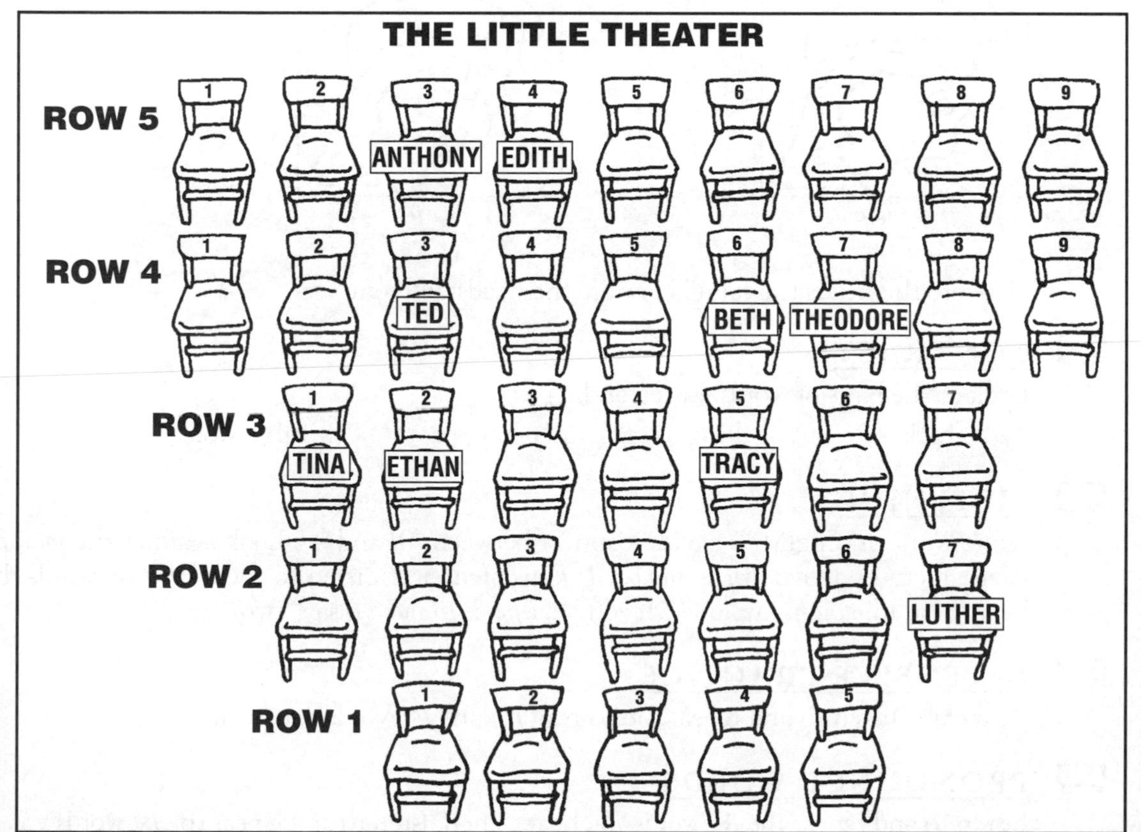

PART TWO /θ/ and /s/

On page 106, you learned about the sound /θ/ (as in the word <u>th</u>*ink*) at the beginning of a word, in the middle of a word, or at the end of a word. In Lesson 9, you learned about the sound /s/ at the beginning of a word, in the middle of a word, or at the end of a word.

Contrasting the Consonants /θ/ and /s/

WARM-UP

Look at the pictures. Listen to the words and repeat them.

1. mouth /θ/

2. mouse /s/

ARTICULATION

Look at the pictures. The heads show how to make the sounds.

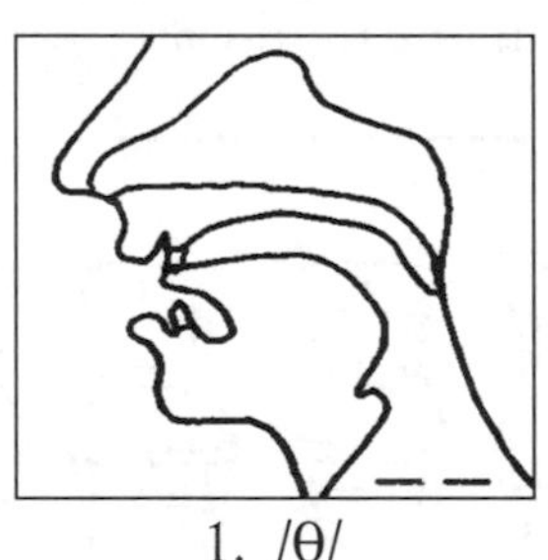

1. /θ/

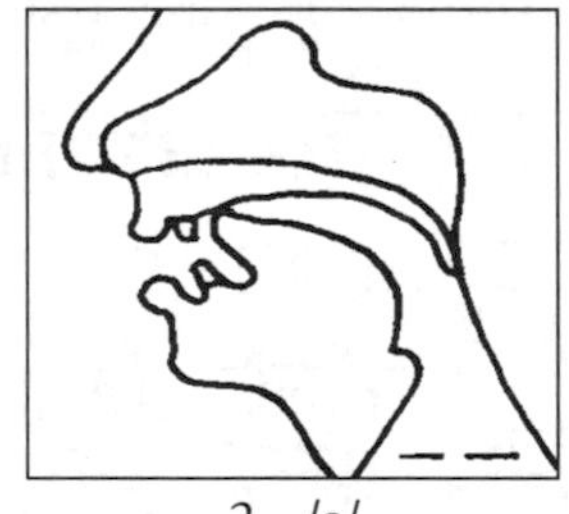

2. /s/

How are the heads the same? How are the heads different?

CONTRAST

Look at the pairs of words. Listen and repeat.

thick – sick　　thing – sing　　path – pass　　worth – worse

LISTENING

Some words in English have the contrast between /θ/ and /s/. Look again at the *mouth* and *mouse* pictures above. /θ/ is *number 1*. /s/ is *number 2*. Listen to the following words. If you hear /θ/ as in *mouth*, say "one." If you hear /s/ as in *mouse*, say "two."

INTENSIVE PRACTICE

As a class, listen to and repeat the pairs of /θ/ and /s/ words you hear.

PRONOUNCE WORDS

Listen to and repeat the /θ/ words you hear. Then listen to and repeat the /s/ words you hear.

PRONOUNCE PHRASES

Listen to and repeat the phrases you hear.

PRONOUNCE SENTENCES

Listen to and repeat the sentences you hear.

PRACTICE ACTIVITIES

PARTNER 1

1a. LISTENING DISCRIMINATION AND SPEAKING. Pair Practice Words for /θ/ and /s/.
PARTNER 1. Use this page. PARTNER 2. Turn to page 121.

DIRECTIONS: First you are the speaker. Say the words to your partner. You see the consonant sound before each word. For example, you say "Number 1 is *sing*." Repeat any words your partner does not understand.

1. /s/ sing
2. /θ/ thumb
3. /θ/ theme
4. /s/ pass
5. /θ/ thick
6. /θ/ tenth
7. /s/ mouse
8. /s/ sank
9. /s/ worse
10. /θ/ think

Now you are the listener. Your partner will say some words. Circle the words you hear. Ask your partner to repeat any words you do not understand. Number 11 is an example.

11. (path) pass
12. worth worse
13. think sink
14. mouth mouse
15. thing sing
16. thank sank
17. thumb some
18. thick sick
19. theme seem
20. tenth tense

Now compare answers with your partner.

PARTNER 1

2a. LISTENING DISCRIMINATION AND SPEAKING. Pair Practice Sentences for /θ/ and /s/.
PARTNER 1. Use this page. PARTNER 2. Turn to page 121.

DIRECTIONS: First you are the speaker. Say the sentences to your partner. You see the consonant sound before each sentence. Repeat any sentences your partner does not understand.

1. /θ/ Why did they THINK it?
2. /θ/ Dan pointed to the MOUTH.
3 /s/ Did you notice her SIGH?
4. /s/ He thinks MASS is important.

Now you are the listener. Your partner will say some sentences. Circle the word you hear. Ask your partner to repeat any sentences you do not understand. Number 5 is an example.

5. Kate is the ________ person in the room.
   a. tenth b. (tense)
6. I don't know how to spell "________ ."
   a. worth b. worse
7. Mine is ________ than yours.
   a. thicker b. sicker
8. The house is near a mountain ________ .
   a. path b. pass

Now compare answers with your partner.

PARTNER 1

3a. SPEAKING AND LISTENING. Pair Practice for /θ/ and /s/. PARTNER 1. Use this page. PARTNER 2. Turn to page 122.

DIRECTIONS: Here are the names of some American stars. Ask your partner about the stars' birthdays. Write the birthdays next to the names. Pronounce /θ/ and /s/ correctly.

EXAMPLE:

YOU: When's Jane Fonda's birthday?
YOUR PARTNER: Her birthday is December twenty-first, nineteen thirty-seven.

Jane Fonda ***December 21, 1937***

1. Clint Eastwood ______
2. Tina Turner ______
3. Elvis Presley ______
4. Michael Jackson ______
5. Jerry Lee Lewis ______
6. Stevie Wonder ______

Here are more names of American stars and their birthdays. Answer your partner's questions. Pronounce /θ/ and /s/ correctly in the names and dates.

EXAMPLE:

YOUR PARTNER: When's Jane Fonda's birthday?
YOU: Her birthday is December twenty-first, nineteen thirty-seven.

7. Paul Simon: October 13, 1941
8. Diana Ross: March 26, 1944
9. Ray Charles: September 23, 1930
10. Frank Sinatra: December 12, 1915
11. Aretha Franklin: March 25, 1942
12. Raquel Welch: September 5, 1940

PART THREE /ð/ and /d/

In English, you find the consonant sound /ð/ (as in the word *the*) at the beginning of a word and in the middle of a word. Only a few words have /ð/ at the end.

Beginning	*Middle*	*End*
them	other	breathe
they	weather	bathe
these	brother	
that	northern	

In Lesson 10, you learned about the sound /d/ at the beginning of a word, in the middle of a word, or at the end of a word.

Contrasting the Consonants /ð/ and /d/

WARM-UP

Look at the pictures. Listen to the words and repeat them.

1. they /ð/

2. day /d/

ARTICULATION

Look at the pictures. The heads show how to make the sounds.

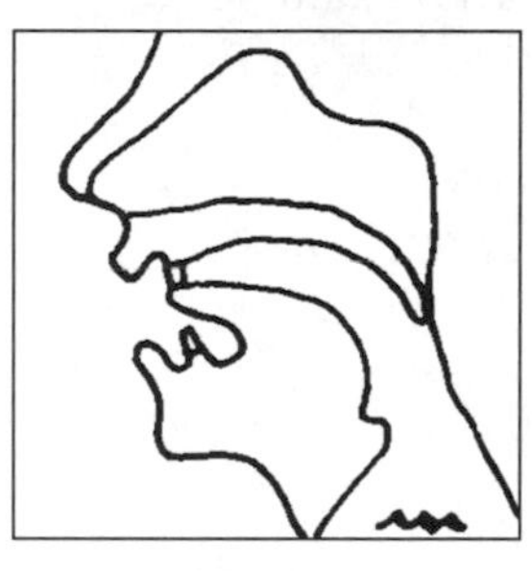

1. /ð/

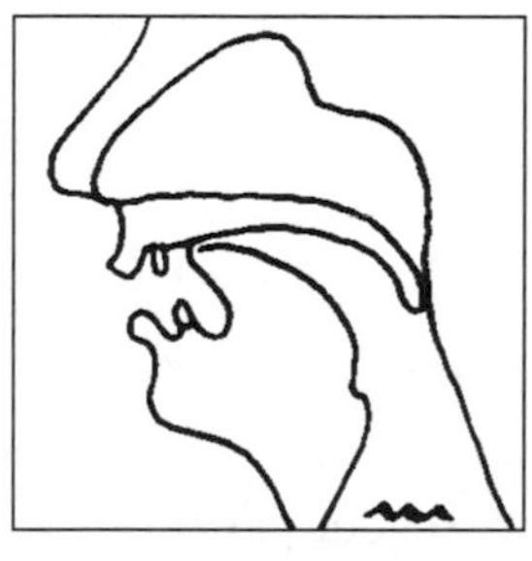

2. /d/

How are the heads the same? How are the heads different?

CONTRAST

Look at the pairs of words. Listen and repeat.

then – den   there – dare   worthy – wordy   than – Dan

LISTENING

Some words in English have the contrast between /ð/ and /d/. Look again at the *they* and *day* pictures above. /ð/ is *number 1.* /d/ is *number 2.* Listen to the following words. If you hear /ð/ as in *they*, say "one." If you hear /d/ as in *day*, say "two."

INTENSIVE PRACTICE

As a class, listen to and repeat the pairs of /ð/ and /d/ words you hear.

PRONOUNCE WORDS

Listen to and repeat the /ð/ words you hear. Then listen to and repeat the /d/ words you hear.

PRONOUNCE PHRASES

Listen to and repeat the phrases you hear.

PRONOUNCE SENTENCES

Listen to and repeat the sentences you hear.

PRACTICE ACTIVITIES

PARTNER 1

1a. LISTENING DISCRIMINATION AND SPEAKING. Pair Practice Words for /ð/ and /d/.
PARTNER 1. Use this page. PARTNER 2. Turn to page 122.

DIRECTIONS: First you are the speaker. Say the words to your partner. You see the consonant sound before each word. For example, you say "Number 1 is *there*." Repeat any words your partner does not understand.

1. /ð/ there
2. /d/ den
3. /ð/ they
4. /ð/ worthy
5. /ð/ than

Now you are the listener. Your partner will say some words. Circle the words you hear. Ask your partner to repeat any words you do not understand. Number 6 is an example.

6. (worthy) wordy
7. than Dan
8. they day
9. there dare
10. then den

Now compare answers with your partner.

PARTNER 1

2a. LISTENING DISCRIMINATION AND SPEAKING. Pair Practice Sentences for /ð/ and /d/.
PARTNER 1. Use this page. PARTNER 2. Turn to page 123.

DIRECTIONS: First you are the speaker. Say the sentences to your partner. You see the consonant sound before each sentence. Repeat any sentences your partner does not understand.

1. /d/ Did you say "DAN?"
2. /ð/ What did you do to THIS COVER?
3. /ð/ The book is WORTHY.
4. /d/ When will DAY come?

Now you are the listener. Your partner will say some sentences. Circle the word you hear. Ask your partner to repeat any sentences you do not understand. Number 5 is an example.

5. Did you say "____________"?
   a. (there) b. dare
6. Your report was ____________ .
   a. worthy b. wordy
7. How do you spell "____________"?
   a. they b. day
8. What did you do to ____________ ?
   a. this side b. decide

Now compare answers with your partner.

PARTNER 1

3a. LISTENING DISCRIMINATION AND SPEAKING. **Challenge! Pair Practice for /ð/ and /d/. PARTNER 1. Use this page. PARTNER 2. Turn to page 123.

DIRECTIONS: Say these negative sentences. Pronounce /ð/ and /d/ correctly. Your partner will agree and use the word *either*.

EXAMPLE:

YOU:	I don't have twenty dollars in my pocket.
YOUR PARTNER:	I don't either.
YOU:	They didn't drink milk.
YOUR PARTNER:	We didn't either.

1. I don't have a dictionary.
2. They don't understand this lesson.
3. I didn't do the laundry.
4. I don't study on Saturday.
5. They didn't go to the movies together.
6. I didn't dance at the party.

Now listen to your partner's negative sentences. Agree and use the word *either*. Respond with *I* or *we*. Listen carefully to your partner's sentences. Some of them are in the present tense. Some of them are in the past tense. Be sure to pronounce /ð/ in *either* and /d/ in *don't* and *didn't*.

EXAMPLE:

YOUR PARTNER:	I didn't have a car accident.
YOU:	I didn't either.
YOUR PARTNER:	They don't like to eat candy.
YOU:	We don't either.

4. REPORT. Group or Class Presentations to Practice /ð/.

DIRECTIONS: Tell the other students in your group or class about one of your friends or family. Talk for three to four minutes. Tell the class how your friend or family member is different from you.

EXAMPLE:

My best friend Daniel is taller than me. His hair is darker than my hair. He is younger than me. He plays baseball better than me . . . .

PART FOUR /ð/ and /z/

On page 112 you read about the sound /ð/ (as in the word *the*) at the beginning of a word and in the middle of a word. In Lesson 9 you read about the sound /z/ in the middle of a word or at the end of a word.

Contrasting the Consonants /ð/ and /z/

WARM-UP

Look at the pictures. Listen to the words and repeat them.

1. clothing /ð/

2. closing /z/

ARTICULATION

Look at the pictures. The heads show how to make the sounds.

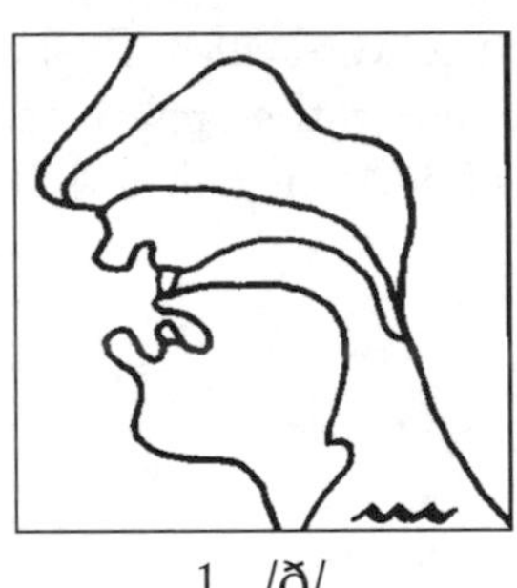

1. /ð/

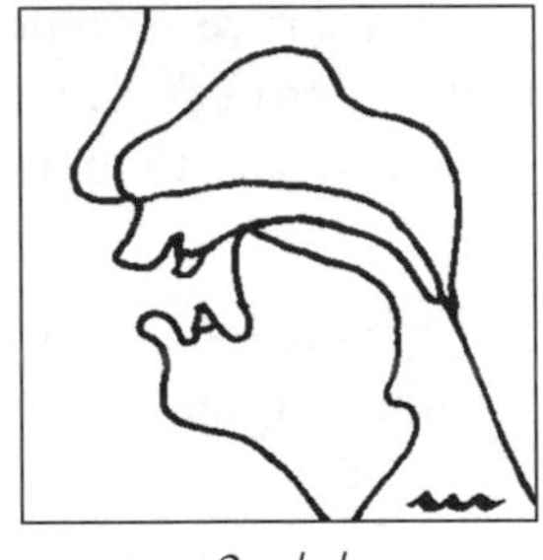

2. /z/

How are the heads the same? How are the heads different?

CONTRAST

Look at the pairs of words. Listen and repeat.

the – Z　　breathe – breeze　　teethe – tease

LISTENING

A few words in English have the contrast between /ð/ and /z/. Look again at the *clothing* and *closing* pictures above. /ð/ is *number 1*. /z/ is *number 2*. Listen to the following words. If you hear /ð/ as in *clothing*, say "one." If you hear /z/ as in *closing*, say "two."

INTENSIVE PRACTICE

As a class, listen to and repeat the pairs of /ð/ and /z/ words you hear.

PRONOUNCE WORDS

Listen to and repeat the /ð/ words you hear. Then listen to and repeat the /z/ words you hear.

PRONOUNCE PHRASES

Listen to and repeat the phrases you hear.

PRONOUNCE SENTENCES

Listen to and repeat the sentences you hear.

PRACTICE ACTIVITIES

PARTNER 1

1a. LISTENING DISCRIMINATION AND SPEAKING. Pair Practice Words for /ð/ and /z/. PARTNER 1. Use this page. PARTNER 2. Turn to page 124.

DIRECTIONS: First you are the speaker. Say the words to your partner. You see the consonant sound before each word. For example, you say "Number 1 is *closing*." Repeat any words your partner does not understand.

1. /z/ closing
2. /ð/ breathe
3. /ð/ then
4. /z/ tease
5. /z/ Z

Now you are the listener. Your partner will say some words. Circle the words you hear. Ask your partner to repeat any words you do not understand. Number 6 is an example.

6.	(teethe)	tease	9.	the	Z
7.	clothing	closing	10.	breathe	breeze
8.	then	Zen			

Now compare answers with your partner.

PARTNER 1

2a. INTERVIEW. Pair Practice for /ð/ and /z/. PARTNER 1. Use this page. PARTNER 2. Turn to page 124.

DIRECTIONS: You will tell the class about your partner's hometown. You need some information. Write the name of your partner's home town on the line. Then ask your partner about the places on the list. Pronounce /ð/ and /z/ correctly. Check "yes" or "no" after your partner answers.

EXAMPLE:
travel service ✓ yes ___ no
YOU: Is there a travel service in your home town?
YOUR PARTNER: Yes, there is.
My partner's home town is ____________________ .

PLACES

1.	movie theater	___ yes	___ no	4.	doctor's office	___ yes	___ no
2.	museum	___ yes	___ no	5.	amusement park	___ yes	___ no
3.	hospital	___ yes	___ no	6.	newsstand	___ yes	___ no

Next your partner will ask you about your home town. Answer with "Yes, there is" or "No, there isn't." Pronounce /ð/ and /z/ correctly.

EXAMPLE: YOUR PARTNER: Is there an art center in your home town?
YOU: Yes, there is.

Now tell the class about your partner's home town. Use "There's . . ." and "There isn't . . ."

EXAMPLE: YOU: My partner's home town is Chicago. There's a travel service . . .

3. SPEAKING. Pair or Group Practice for /ð/ and /z/. This is a picture of a family tree.

DIRECTIONS: Take turns asking and answering questions about the family tree. You and your group need to pronounce /ð/ and /z/ clearly.

EXAMPLES:

STUDENT 1: Who's Elizabeth's mother?

STUDENT 2: Elizabeth's mother is Heather. Who's James?

STUDENT 3: James is Rose's brother. Who's . . .

4. SPEAKING. Whose is this? Class Game to Practice /ð/ and /z/.

DIRECTIONS: Stand up in a circle with your classmates. Your instructor will tell a student to start the game. The first student picks up an object and asks another student, "Whose is this?" The second student answers.

EXAMPLES:

STUDENT 1: (*Picks up a calculator*) Whose is this?

STUDENT 2: That's Karen's. *(Picks up a notebook)* Whose is this?

STUDENT 3: That's Lim's. . . .

Some objects can be plural *(glasses, pens)*. For plural objects, be sure to use "Whose are these?" and answer "Those are . . ."

PARTNER 2

1b. LISTENING DISCRIMINATION AND SPEAKING. Pair Practice Words for /θ/ and /t/.
PARTNER 2. Use this page. PARTNER 1. Turn to page 108.

DIRECTIONS: First you are the listener. Your partner will say some words. Circle the words you hear. Ask your partner to repeat any words you do not understand. Number 1 is an example.

1. (theme) team
2. thigh tie
3. math mat
4. threw true
5. both boat
6. thin tin
7. thought taught
8. tenth tent
9. booth boot
10. three tree

Now you are the speaker. Say the words to your partner. You see the consonant sound before each word. For example, you say "Number 11 is *tenth*." Repeat any words your partner does not understand.

11. /θ/ tenth
12. /t/ boot
13. /θ/ thought
14. /θ/ math
15. /t/ tree
16. /θ/ thank
17. /t/ true
18. /t/ boat
19. /t/ tie
20. /θ/ thin

Now compare answers with your partner.

PARTNER 2

2b. LISTENING DISCRIMINATION AND SPEAKING. Pair Practice Sentences for /θ/ and /t/.
PARTNER 2. Use this page. PARTNER 1. Turn to page 108.

DIRECTIONS: First you are the listener. Your partner will say some sentences. Circle the word you hear. Ask your partner to repeat any sentences you do not understand. Number 1 is an example.

1. Bob spilled coffee on his __________ .
   a. thigh b. (tie)
2. Which one is your __________ ?
   a. theme b. team
3. They want money for __________ .
   a. thanks b. tanks
4. Is it __________ ?
   a. through b. true

Now you are the speaker. Say the sentences to your partner. You see the consonant sound before each sentence. Repeat any sentences your partner does not understand.

5. /θ/ I'll use a THIN pan.
6. /θ/ This is no place for a BATH.
7. /t/ Joe TAUGHT for many years.
8. /t/ You can't fit in this BOOT.

Now compare answers with your partner.

PARTNER 2

3b. SPEAKING AND LISTENING. Pair Practice for /θ/ and /t/. PARTNER 2. Use this page. PARTNER 1. Turn to page 109.

DIRECTIONS: Here is the Little Theater. Your partner wants to buy a ticket for tomorrow's performance. Your partner will ask you where his or her friends are going to sit. Tell your partner what *row* and *seat* each person is going to sit in. Pronounce /θ/ and /t/ correctly.

EXAMPLE:

YOUR PARTNER: Where's Thelma going to sit?
YOU: Thelma's going to sit in the third row in the fourth seat.

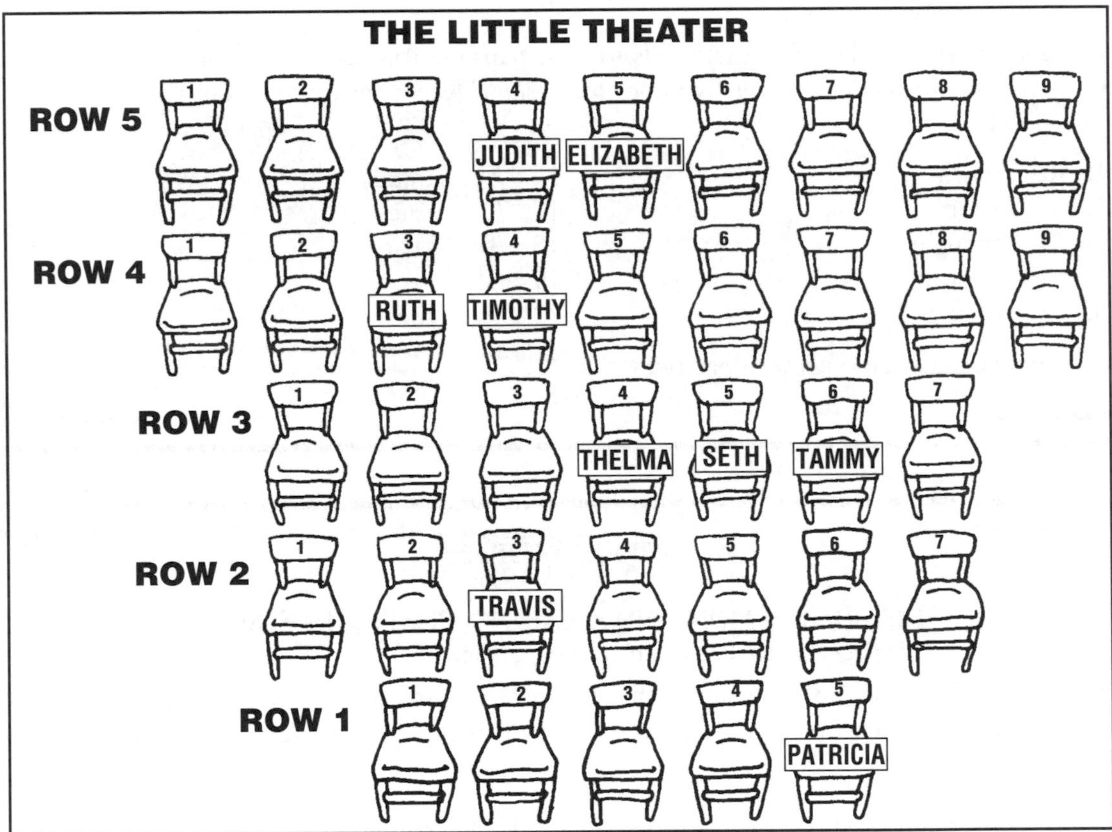

Now you want to buy a ticket for next week at the Little Theater. You want to sit near one of your friends on the list. Ask your partner where your friends are going to sit. Pronounce /θ/ and /t/ correctly.

EXAMPLE:

YOU: Where's Anthony going to sit?
YOUR PARTNER: Anthony's going to sit in the fifth row in the third seat.

FRIENDS

Anthony	Tina	Tracy
Beth	Theodore	Ted
Luther	Edith	Ethan

PARTNER 2

1b. LISTENING DISCRIMINATION AND SPEAKING. Pair Practice Words for /θ/ and /s/.
PARTNER 2. Use this page. PARTNER 1. Turn to page 111.

DIRECTIONS: First you are the listener. Your partner will say some words. Circle the words you hear. Ask your partner to repeat any words you do not understand. Number 1 is an example.

1. thing (sing)
2. thumb some
3. theme seem
4. path pass
5. thick sick
6. tenth tense
7. mouth mouse
8. thank sank
9. worth worse
10. think sink

Now you are the speaker. Say the words to your partner. You see the consonant sound before each word. For example, you say "Number 11 is *path*." Repeat any words your partner does not understand.

11. /θ/ path
12. /s/ worse
13. /s/ sink
14. /θ/ mouth
15. /θ/ thing
16. /θ/ thank
17. /s/ some
18. /s/ sick
19. /s/ seem
20. /θ/ tenth

Now compare answers with your partner.

PARTNER 2

2b. LISTENING DISCRIMINATION AND SPEAKING. Pair Practice Sentences for /θ/ and /s/.
PARTNER 2. Use this page. PARTNER 1. Turn to page 111.

DIRECTIONS: First you are the listener. Your partner will say some sentences. Circle the word you hear. Ask your partner to repeat any sentences you do not understand. Number 1 is an example.

1. Why did they ______________ it?
   a. (think) b. sink
2. Dan pointed to the ____________ .
   a. mouth b. mouse
3. Did you notice her ______________ ?
   a. thigh b. sigh
4. He thinks ___________ is important.
   a. math b. mass

Now you are the speaker. Say the sentences to your partner. You see the consonant sound before each sentence. Repeat any sentences your partner does not understand.

5. /s/ Kate is the TENSE person in the room.
6. /θ/ I don't know how to spell "WORTH."
7. /θ/ Mine is THICKER than yours.
8. /s/ The house is near a mountain PASS.

Now compare answers with your partner.

PARTNER 2

3b. SPEAKING AND LISTENING. Pair Practice for /θ/ and /s/. PARTNER 2. Use this page. PARTNER 1. Turn to page 112.

DIRECTIONS: Here are the names of some American stars and their birthdays. Answer your partner's questions. Pronounce /θ/ and /s/ correctly in the names and dates.

EXAMPLE:

YOUR PARTNER: When's Jane Fonda's bir<u>th</u>day?
YOU: Her bir<u>th</u>day is De<u>c</u>ember twenty-first, nineteen <u>th</u>irty <u>s</u>even.

1. Clint Eastwood: May 31, 1930
2. Tina Turner: November 26, 1938
3. Elvis Presley: January 8, 1935
4. Michael Jackson: August 29, 1958
5. Jerry Lee Lewis: September 29, 1935
6. Stevie Wonder: May 3, 1950

Here are more names of American stars. Ask your partner about the stars' birthdays. Write the birthdays next to the names. Pronounce /θ/ and /s/ correctly.

EXAMPLE:

YOU: When's Jane Fonda's bir<u>th</u>day?
YOUR PARTNER: Her bir<u>th</u>day is De<u>c</u>ember twenty-fir<u>s</u>t, nineteen <u>th</u>irty <u>s</u>even.

Jane Fonda ***December 21, 1937***

7. Paul Simon ______________________
8. Diana Ross ______________________
9. Ray Charles ______________________
10. Frank Sinatra ______________________
11. Aretha Franklin ______________________
12. Raquel Welch ______________________

PARTNER 2

1b. LISTENING DISCRIMINATION AND SPEAKING. Pair Practice Words for /ð/ and /d/. PARTNER 2. Use this page. PARTNER 1. Turn to page 114.

DIRECTIONS: First you are the listener. Your partner will say some words. Circle the words you hear. Ask your partner to repeat any words you do not understand. Number 1 is an example.

1. (there) dare
2. then den
3. they day
4. worthy wordy
5. than Dan

Now you are the speaker. Say the words to your partner. You see the consonant sound before each word. For example, you say "Number 6 is *worthy*." Repeat any words your partner does not understand.

6. /ð/ worthy
7. /d/ Dan
8. /ð/ they
9. /ð/ there
10. /ð/ then

Now compare answers with your partner.

PARTNER 2

2b. LISTENING DISCRIMINATION AND SPEAKING. Pair Practice Sentences for /ð/ and /d/. PARTNER 2. Use this page. PARTNER 1. Turn to page 114.

DIRECTIONS: First you are the listener. Your partner will say some sentences. Circle the word you hear. Ask your partner to repeat any sentences you do not understand. Number 1 is an example.

1. Did you say "__________"?
   a. than b. (Dan)
2. What did you do to __________ ?
   a. this cover b. discover
3. The book is __________ .
   a. worthy b. wordy
4. When will __________ come?
   a. they b. day

Now you are the speaker. Say the sentences to your partner. You see the consonant sound before each sentence. Repeat any sentences your partner does not understand.

5. /ð/ Did you say "THERE"?
6. /d/ Your report was WORDY.
7. /d/ How do you spell "DAY"?
8. /ð/ What did you do to THIS SIDE?

Now compare answers with your partner.

PARTNER 2

3b. LISTENING DISCRIMINATION AND SPEAKING. **Challenge! Pair Practice for /ð/ and /d/. PARTNER 2. Use this page. PARTNER 1. Turn to page 115.

DIRECTIONS: Listen to your partner's negative sentences. Agree and use the word *either*. Respond with *I* or *we*. Listen carefully to your partner's sentences. Some of them are in the present tense. Some of them are in the past tense. Be sure to pronounce /ð/ in *either* and /d/ in *don't* and *didn't*.

EXAMPLE:

YOUR PARTNER:	I don't have twenty dollars in my pocket.
YOU:	I don't either.
YOUR PARTNER:	They didn't drink milk.
YOU:	We didn't either.

Now say these negative sentences. Pronounce /ð/ and /d/ correctly. Your partner will agree and use the word *either*.

EXAMPLE:

YOU:	I didn't have a car accident.
YOUR PARTNER:	I didn't either.
YOU:	They don't like to eat candy.
YOUR PARTNER:	We don't either.

7. I don't spend a lot of money.
8. They don't drive to work on Mondays.
9. I don't do homework every weekend.
10. I didn't send a letter to my friend.
11. They didn't buy their medicine at a drugstore.
12. I don't have a headache today.

PAIR PRACTICE: Partner 2

PARTNER 2

1b. LISTENING DISCRIMINATION AND SPEAKING. Pair Practice Words for /ð/ and /z/. PARTNER 2. Use this page. PARTNER 1. Turn to page 117.

DIRECTIONS: First you are the listener. Your partner will say some words. Circle the words you hear. Ask your partner to repeat any words you do not understand. Number 1 is an example.

1 clothing (closing)
2. breathe breeze
3. then Zen
4. teethe tease
5. the Z

Now you are the speaker. Say the words to your partner. You can see the consonant sound you need to pronounce. For example, you say "Number 6 is *teethe*." Repeat any words your partner does not understand.

6. /ð/ teethe
7. /ð/ clothing
8. /z/ Zen
9. /ð/ the
10. /ð/ breathe

Now compare answers with your partner.

PARTNER 2

2b. INTERVIEW. Pair Practice for /ð/ and /z/. PARTNER 2. Use this page. PARTNER 1. Turn to page 117.

DIRECTIONS: Your partner will ask you about your home town. Answer with "Yes, there is" or "No, there isn't." Pronounce /ð/ and /z/ correctly.

EXAMPLE: YOUR PARTNER: Is there a travel service in your home town?
YOU: Yes, there is.

Next, you will tell the class about your partner's home town. You need some information. Write the name of your partner's home town on the line. Then ask your partner about the places on the list. Pronounce /ð/ and /z/ correctly. Check "yes" or "no" after your partner answers.

EXAMPLE:
art center ✓ yes ___ no
YOU: Is there an art center in your home town?
YOUR PARTNER: Yes, there is.
My partner's home town is ____________________ .

PLACES

1. gymnasium ___ yes ___ no
2. library ___ yes ___ no
3. post office ___ yes ___ no
4. zoo ___ yes ___ no
5. health clinic ___ yes ___ no
6. music school ___ yes ___ no

Now tell the class about your partner's home town. Use "There's . . ." and "There isn't . . ."

EXAMPLE: YOU: My partner's home town is Denver. There's an art center . . .

LESSON **12**

The Consonants /tʃ/ and /dʒ/

PART ONE /tʃ/ and /ʃ/

In English, you find the consonant sound /tʃ/ (as in the word *chair*) at the beginning of a word, in the middle of a word, or at the end of a word.

Beginning	*Middle*	*End*
check	kitchen	catch
child	teacher	each
change	future	much
cheese	watching	lunch

You can find the sound /ʃ/ (as in the word *show*) at the beginning of a word, in the middle of a word, or at the end of a word, too.

Beginning	*Middle*	*End*
she	washer	dish
short	machine	push
shoe	nation	finish
shop	fishing	English

Contrasting the Consonants /tʃ/ and /ʃ/

WARM-UP

Look at the pictures. Listen to the words and repeat them.

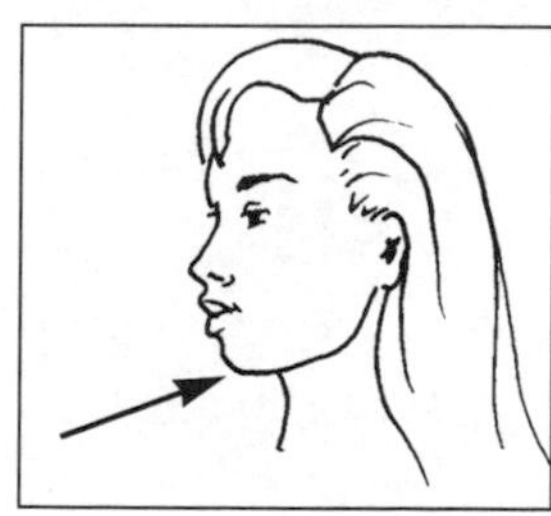

1. chin /tʃ/

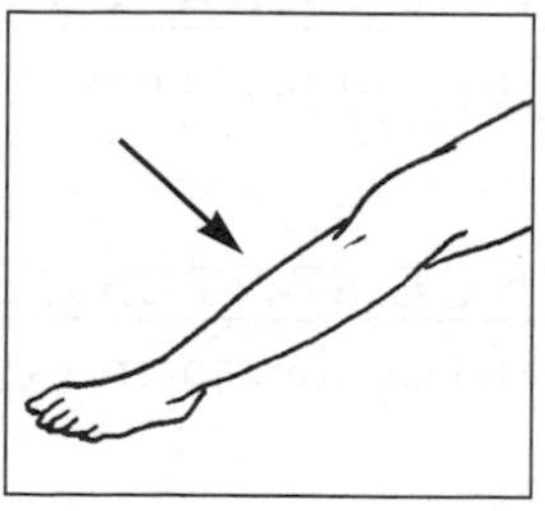

2. shin /ʃ/

ARTICULATION

Look at the pictures. The heads show how to make the sounds.

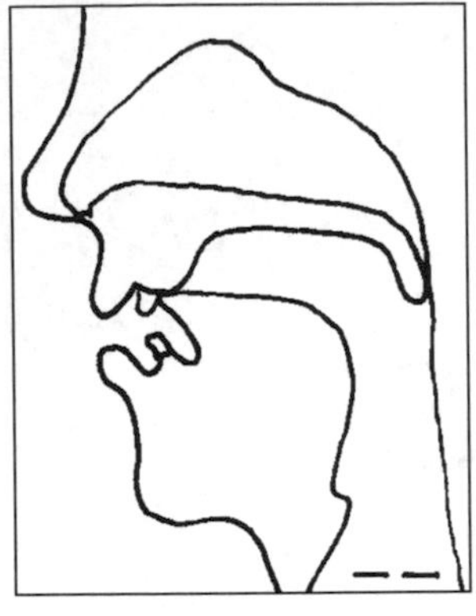

1. /tʃ/ a.

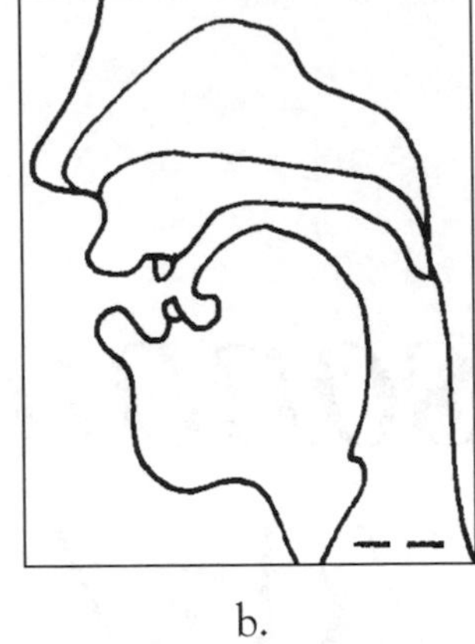

b.

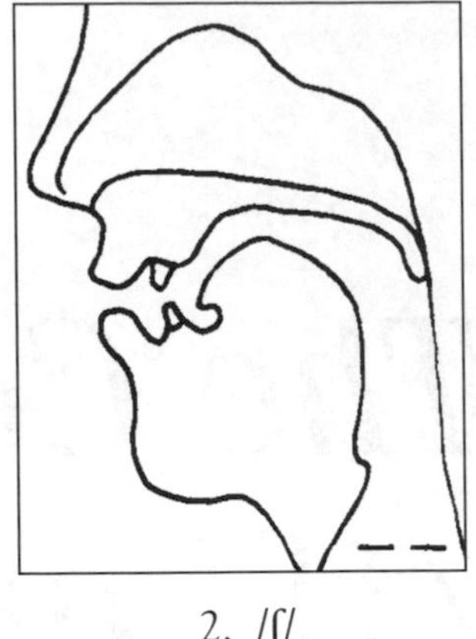

2. /ʃ/

How is their pronunciation the same? How is their pronunciation different?

CONTRAST

Look at the pairs of words. Listen and repeat.

chew – shoe

cheap – sheep

cheese – she's

watch – wash

LISTENING

Many words in English have the contrast between /tʃ/ and /ʃ/. Look again at the *chin* and *shin* pictures on page 125. /tʃ/ is *number 1.* /ʃ/ is *number 2.* Listen to the following words. If you hear /tʃ/ as in *chin*, say "one." If you hear /ʃ/ as in *shin*, say "two."

INTENSIVE PRACTICE

As a class, listen to and repeat the pairs of /tʃ/ and /ʃ/ words you hear.

PRONOUNCE WORDS

Listen to and repeat the /tʃ/ words you hear. Then listen to and repeat the /ʃ/ words you hear.

PRONOUNCE PHRASES

Listen to and repeat the phrases you hear.

PRONOUNCE SENTENCES

Listen to and repeat the sentences you hear.

PRACTICE ACTIVITIES

PARTNER 1

1a. LISTENING DISCRIMINATION AND SPEAKING. Pair Practice Words for /tʃ/ and /ʃ/.
PARTNER 1. Use this page. PARTNER 2. Turn to page 138.

DIRECTIONS: First you are the speaker. Say the words to your partner. You see the consonant sound before each word. For example, you say "Number 1 is *chop*." Repeat any words your partner does not understand.

1. /tʃ/ chop
2. /tʃ/ choose
3. /ʃ/ wash
4. /ʃ/ she's
5. /ʃ/ ship
6. /tʃ/ chin
7. /ʃ/ cash
8. /ʃ/ sheet
9. /tʃ/ which
10. /tʃ/ cheap

Now you are the listener. Your partner will say some words. Circle the words you hear. Ask your partner to repeat any words you do not understand. Number 11 is an example.

11. chin (shin)
12. cheese she's
13. which wish
14. chose shows
15. cheap sheep
16. catch cash
17. chop shop
18. watch wash
19. cheat sheet
20. choose shoes

Now compare answers with your partner.

PARTNER 1

2a. LISTENING DISCRIMINATION AND SPEAKING. Pair Practice Sentences for /tʃ/ and /ʃ/.
PARTNER 1. Use this page. PARTNER 2. Turn to page 138.

DIRECTIONS: First you are the speaker. Say the sentences to your partner. You see the consonant sound before each sentence. Repeat any sentences your partner does not understand.

1. /tʃ/ The man is WATCHING the car.
2. /tʃ/ Can you spell "CHEESE"?
3. /ʃ/ The ball hit her SHIN.
4. /ʃ/ This is a SHEEP blanket.

Now you are the listener. Your partner will say some sentences. Circle the word you hear. Ask your partner to repeat any sentences you do not understand. Number 5 is an example.

5. He always __________ the answer.
   a. chose b. (shows)
6. Please __________ this for me.
   a. catch b. cash
7. How do you spell "__________" ?
   a. which b. wish
8. She doesn't want __________ .
   a. to choose b. two shoes

Now compare answers with your partner.

3. SPEAKING. Guided Conversation to Practice /tʃ/ and /ʃ/.

DIRECTIONS: Imagine that you are going shopping in a sporting goods shop. Here is a list of things you want to buy. Take turns asking for and giving the prices of the things on your list. You and your partner need to pronounce /tʃ/ and /ʃ/ correctly.

EXAMPLE:

SHOPPER: Can I ask you a question?
CASHIER: Sure.
SHOPPER: How much are the golf shoes?
CASHIER: They're sixty dollars.
SHOPPER: Thanks, but that's too much!

SHOPPING LIST

catcher's mitt	*$39*
golf shoes	*$60*
tennis shorts	*$37*
beach chair	*$14*
fishing boots	*$160*
punching bag	*$125*
rowing machine	*$300*
diver's watch	*$97*
bowling shirt	*$31*
running shoes	*$80*

MODEL CONVERSATION

SHOPPER: Can I ask you a question?
CASHIER: Sure.
SHOPPER: How much is / are the ______________________________ ?
CASHIER: It's / They're _______________ dollars.
SHOPPER: Thanks, but that's too much!

PARTNER 1

4a. SPEAKING AND LISTENING. Pair Practice for /tʃ/ and /ʃ/. PARTNER 1. Use this page. PARTNER 2. Turn to page 139.

DIRECTIONS: Here is a page from the Monday evening TV listing.Your partner will ask you about the shows, show times, and channels. Use the TV listing to answer. Pronounce /tʃ/ and /ʃ/ correctly.

EXAMPLE:

YOUR PARTNER: When is *A Shot in the Dark* showing?
YOU: It's showing at 7 o'clock.
YOUR PARTNER: What channel is it on?
YOU: It's on channel 5.

TV LISTING - SHOWS FOR THIS WEEK - MONDAY

Time	Channel	Show	Time	Channel	Show
6:00 PM	2	Newswatch	8:00 PM	2	Movie: *Gold Rush Days*
	5	A Talk with the Nation		52	International News
	9	Charles in Charge	9:00 PM	5	Changing Times
7:00 PM	5	Movie: *A Shot in the Dark*		7	Movie: *Checkmate*
	7	Cheer Up		11	Too Much, Too Soon
	11	Movie: *Modern Professions*		28	News with Chuck Day and Betty Short
	32	Home Shopping Club			
7:30 PM	2	$1,000 March for Cash	10:00 PM	2	WHNW News and Short Reports
	1	Asher and Bush Hour		7	News with Sharon Chad
	6	America's National Parks			
	32	Brush Up Your English			

DIRECTIONS: Now your partner has a page from the Tuesday evening TV listing. Here is a list of TV shows. Ask your partner about times and channels of shows you want to watch. Pronounce /tʃ/ and /ʃ/ correctly.

EXAMPLE:

YOU: When is *Scotch on the Rocks* showing?
YOUR PARTNER: It's showing at eight o'clock.
YOU: What channel is it on?
YOUR PARTNER: It's on channel 11.

TV SHOWS

News
WHNW News Evening Edition
News with Chapman and Shumaker
National News and Sports
News with Chester and Shipp

Variety
The Shawnie Rich Show
Catch the Stars

Recreation
Adventure on the Ocean

Movies
Scotch on the Rocks
Checkmate
Out of Touch
Teach Me Tonight
Picture It

Game Shows
Get Rich Quick
Spin for Fortune

Education
Nature

Series
Shootout
The Sheriff
On the Shelf

Documentary
Change in Chinatown

5. INTERVIEW. Pair Practice for /tʃ/ and /ʃ/.

DIRECTIONS: Interview a partner about a TV show he or she watched. You can take notes to help you remember. You need to know the name of the show, the day, the time, and the channel. Find out what happened on the show. Find out if your partner liked the show.

Your partner will interview you, too. Choose who will ask or answer first. After the interviews, tell the other students in the class about the TV show your partner watched. You can use your notes from the interview. When you speak to the class about your partner, pronounce /tʃ/ and /ʃ/ correctly.

SPELLING

FIGURE IT OUT

Here are some words with the sounds /tʃ/ and /ʃ/ at the beginning and end. Study the spelling of these words.

/tʃ/	/ʃ/
chair	she
child	sharp
rich	fish
beach	finish
watch	push
match	English

What letters make the sound /tʃ/ at the beginning of a word? How about at the end of a word? Write some spelling rules.

RULE FOR /tʃ/ AT THE BEGINNING AND END OF WORDS

1. At the beginning of a word, you can spell the sound /tʃ/ with the letters ____ ____ .
2. At the end of a word, you can spell the sound /tʃ/ with the letters ____ ____ or the letters ____ ____ ____ .

What letters make the sound /ʃ/ at the beginning or end of a word? Write a spelling rule.

RULE FOR /ʃ/ AT THE BEGINNING OR END OF WORDS

At the beginning or end of a word, you can spell the sound /ʃ/ with the letters ____ ____ .

You can find /tʃ/ and /ʃ/ in the middle of words. Sometimes, they are spelled the same as at the beginning and end.

/tʃ/	/ʃ/
kitchen	cashier
teacher	washer
exchange	freshman

There are many different ways to spell these sounds in the middle of a word, too. Now here are some words with the sounds /tʃ/ and /ʃ/ in the middle. Study the spelling of these words.

/tʃ/	/ʃ/
question	vacation
suggestion	station
future	addition
picture	mission
natural	profession
furniture	pressure

What letters make the sound /tʃ/ in the middle of a word? Write some spelling rules.

RULES FOR /tʃ/ IN THE MIDDLE OF WORDS

1. In the middle of a word, you can spell the sound /tʃ/ with *s* + the letters ____ ____ ____ ____ .
2. In the middle of a word, you can spell the sound /tʃ/ with the letters ____ ____ .

What letters make the sound /ʃ/ in the middle of a word? Write some spelling rules.

RULES FOR /ʃ/ IN THE MIDDLE OF WORDS

1. In the middle of a word, you can spell the sound /ʃ/ with a vowel + the letters ____ ____ ____ ____ .
2. In the middle of a word, you can spell the sound /ʃ/ with two _____ + *ion* or *ure.*

There are some exceptions to these rules. Listen to your instructor say these /ʃ/ words:

sure, sugar, special, delicious, machine, Chicago, Michigan, ocean

PART TWO /tʃ/ and /dʒ/

On page 125, you read about the sound /tʃ/ (as in the word *children*) at the beginning of a word, in the middle of a word, or at the end of a word.

In English, you find the consonant sound /dʒ/ (as in the word *job*) at the beginning of a word, in the middle of a word, or at the end of a word, too.

Beginning	*Middle*	*End*
job	magic	age
juice	danger	large
jeans	subject	postage
gym	engine	package

Contrasting the Consonants /tʃ/ and /dʒ/

WARM-UP

Look at the pictures. Listen to the words and repeat them.

1. cello /tʃ/

2. jello /dʒ/

ARTICULATION

Look at the pictures. The heads show how to make the sounds.

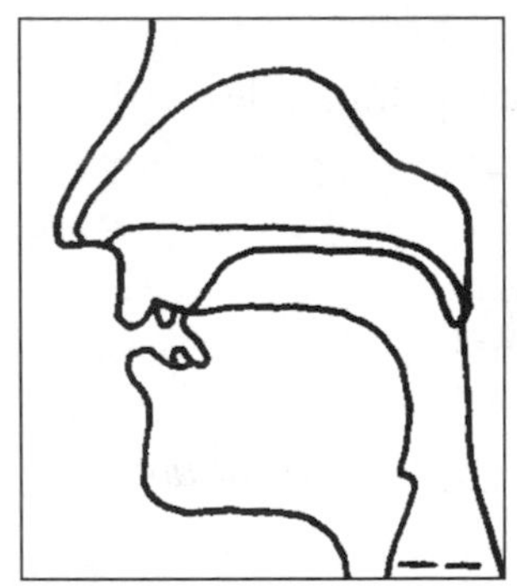

1. /tʃ/ a. b.

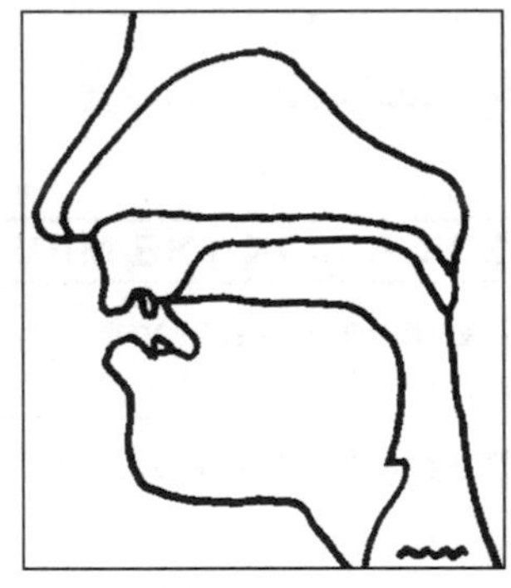

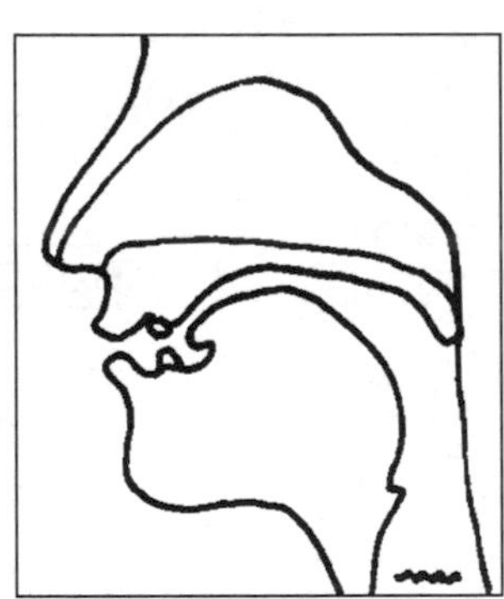

2. /dʒ/ a. b.

How are the heads the same? How are the heads different?

CONTRAST

Look at the pairs of words. Listen and repeat.

cheap – jeep
chain – Jane
choke – joke
H – age

LISTENING

Some words in English have the contrast between /tʃ/ and /dʒ/. Look again at the *cello* and *jello* pictures above. /tʃ/ is *number 1.* /dʒ/ is *number 2.* Listen to the following words. If you hear /tʃ/ as in *cello*, say "one." If you hear /dʒ/ as in *jello*, say "two."

INTENSIVE PRACTICE

As a class, listen to and repeat the pairs of /tʃ/ and /dʒ/ words you hear.

PRONOUNCE WORDS

Listen to and repeat the /tʃ/ words you hear. Then listen to and repeat the /dʒ/ words you hear.

PRONOUNCE PHRASES

Listen to and repeat the phrases you hear.

PRONOUNCE SENTENCES

Listen to and repeat the sentences you hear.

PRACTICE ACTIVITIES

PARTNER 1

1a. SPEAKING AND LISTENING. Pair Practice for /tʃ/ and /dʒ/. PARTNER 1. Use this page. PARTNER 2. Turn to page 140.

DIRECTIONS: Here is a college schedule with information about classes. You need to know what time and where the classes meet. Take turns with your partner asking and answering questions. Pronounce /tʃ/ and /dʒ/ correctly. Write the answers on the schedule.

EXAMPLE:

YOU:	When does Geology meet?
YOUR PARTNER:	It meets Tuesdays and Thursdays from 11 to 2.
YOU:	Where does it meet?
YOUR PARTNER:	In Chaney Hall B–7.

SCHEDULE OF CLASSES - CHAMBERLAIN COLLEGE

Class	Day	Time	Room/Building
Biology	M. W.	1–3	1 Biology Lab
Engineering I	______	______	______
ESL: American Culture	Tu. Th.	3–4:30	307 Chadwick
ESL: Vocabulary Enrichment	______	______	______
Geography	M. T. W. T.	9–10	101 Lecture Hall
Geology	*Tu. Th.*	*11–2*	*B–7 Chaney Hall*
Gymnastics	M. W.	2–3:30	104 Gym
Journalism	______	______	______
Management	Th.	7–10 PM	322 Church Hall
Physical Education	Daily	4–5	117 Gym
Psychology I	Tu. Th.	9–12	700 Chester
Sociology	______	______	______
Speech Communication	W. F.	12–2	100 Chadwick

Now compare answers with your partner.

2. ROLE-PLAY. Food by Phone. Pair Practice for /tʃ/ and /dʒ/. Here is a menu.

DIRECTIONS: Take turns as the employee and the customer. The customer wants to order food for home delivery. The employee needs to take the order on the phone.

EXAMPLE:

EMPLOYEE: Chuck's Food By Phone. May I help you?
CUSTOMER: Yes. I'd like to place an order.
EMPLOYEE: OK.
CUSTOMER: I'd like a medium pizza.
EMPLOYEE: Do you want any toppings?
CUSTOMER: I want double cheese and sausage.
EMPLOYEE: Do you want something to drink?
CUSTOMER: Two chocolate shakes.
EMPLOYEE: Dessert?
CUSTOMER: No, thanks.
EMPLOYEE: OK, that's a medium pizza with double cheese and sausage and two chocolate shakes. We can deliver in 30 minutes.
CUSTOMER: Thanks!

CHUCK'S FOOD BY PHONE - HOME DELIVERY MENU

PIZZA	Individual	Small	Medium	Large
	$2.99	$4.99	$6.99	$8.99

Choice of Toppings (add $.50 for each)
cheese, double cheese, sausage, artichoke hearts, vegetarian

DESSERTS Peach pie $1.49 Cherry pie $1.49 Chocolate cake $1.29

BEVERAGES Cherry Coke Small $.89 Large $1.29
Chocolate shake $1.49

SPELLING

FIGURE IT OUT

On pages 130-131, you figured out some rules for spelling /tʃ/. Here are some words with the sounds /dʒ/ at the beginning, in the middle, and at the end. Study the spelling of these words.

/dʒ/ *at the beginning*	/dʒ/ *in the middle*	/dʒ/ *at the end*
juice	enjoy	age
jeans	major	page
gym	magic	college
general	stranger	package
giant	schedule	bridge
	graduate	

What letters make the sound /dʒ/ at the beginning of a word? Write a spelling rule.

RULE FOR /dʒ/ AT THE BEGINNING OF WORDS

At the beginning of a word, you can spell the sound /dʒ/ with the letter ______ or the letter ______ .

What letters make the sound /dʒ/ in the middle of a word? Write a spelling rule.

RULE FOR /dʒ/ IN THE MIDDLE OF WORDS

In the middle of a word, you can spell the sound /dʒ/ with the letter ____ , the letter _____ , or the letters _____ ______ .

What letters make the sound /dʒ/ at the end of a word? Write a spelling rule.

RULE FOR /dʒ/ AT THE END OF WORDS

At the end of a word, you can spell the sound /dʒ/ with the letters _____ _____ or the letters ______ ______ ______ .

PART THREE /dʒ/ and /y/

On page 131, you read about the sound /dʒ/ (as in the word just) at the beginning of a word, in the middle of a word, or at the end of a word.

In English, you find the sound /y/ (as in the word yes) at the beginning of a word, in the middle of a word, or at the end of a word. You find /y/ with a vowel sound. Look at these words.

Beginning	*Middle*	*End (part of a vowel sound)*
yes	beyond	I /ay/
you	cute	see /iy/
young	music	day /ey/
united	million	tie /ay/
		boy /ɔy/

Comparing the Consonants /dʒ/ and /y/

ARTICULATION

Look at the pictures. The heads show how to make the sounds.

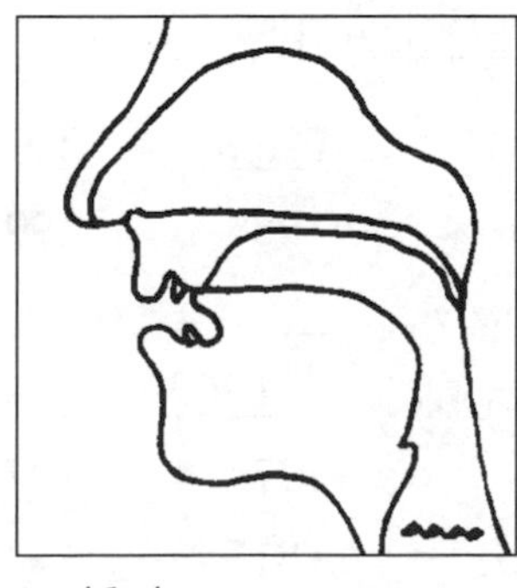

1. /dʒ/ a.

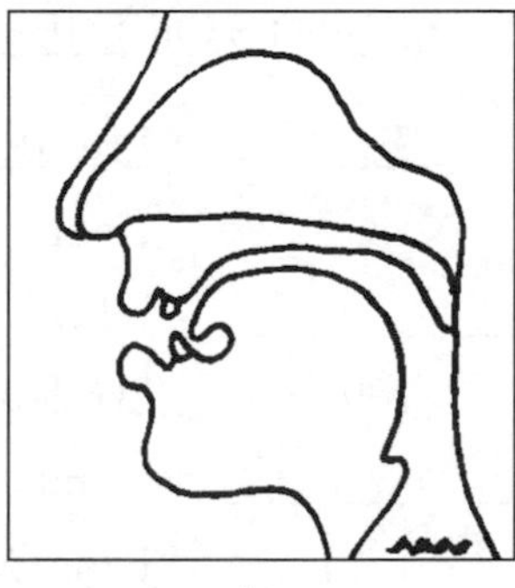

b.

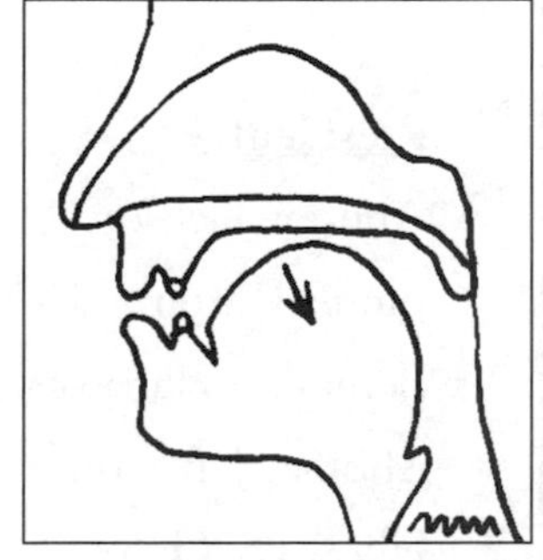

2. /y/

Make the sound /iy/. Your tongue is in the shape for /y/.

Does your tongue touch the roof of your mouth for /dʒ/? How about /y/?

CONTRAST

Look at the pairs of words. Listen and repeat.

jet – yet   juice – use   jewel – you'll   engine – onion

LISTENING

Now look at the pictures on page 135 again. /dʒ/ is *number 1.* /y/ is *number 2.* Listen to the following words. If you hear /dʒ/ as in *jet*, say "one." If you hear /y/ as in *yet*, say "two."

INTENSIVE PRACTICE

As a class, listen to and repeat the pairs of /dʒ/ and /y/ words you hear.

PRONOUNCE WORDS

Listen to and repeat the /dʒ/ words you hear. Then listen to and repeat the /y/ words you hear.

PRONOUNCE PHRASES

Listen to and repeat the phrases you hear.

PRONOUNCE SENTENCES

Listen to and repeat the sentences you hear.

PRACTICE ACTIVITIES

PARTNER 1

1a. SPEAKING AND LISTENING. Pair Practice for /dʒ/ and /y/. PARTNER 1. Use this page. PARTNER 2. Turn to page 141.

DIRECTIONS: Here is information about some presidents of the United States. Take turns asking and answering questions. Write the answers in the chart.

EXAMPLE:

YOU: When was Lyndon Johnson president of the United States?

YOUR PARTNER: Lyndon Johnson was president from 1963 to 1969.

SOME PRESIDENTS OF THE UNITED STATES

President	From	To	President	From	To
Andrew Jackson	1829	1837	George Bush	1988	1992
Jimmy Carter	______	______	John F. Kennedy	______	______
Benjamin Harrison	1889	1893	Lyndon Johnson	***1963***	***1969***
Thomas Jefferson	______	______	Gerald Ford	1974	1977
Ulysses S. Grant	1869	1877	James Monroe	1817	1825
George Washington	______	______	John Adams	______	______

Now compare answers with your partner.

2. INTERVIEW. Pair Practice for /dʒ/ and /y/.

DIRECTIONS: Use the six cues to interview a partner. You can take notes to help you remember your partner's answers.

EXAMPLE:

(CUE): . . . take a vacation in June?
YOU: Do you usually take a vacation in June?

Your partner will interview you, too. Choose who will ask or answer first. After the interviews, tell the other students in the class about your partner. You can use your notes from the interview. When you speak to the class about your partner, pronounce /dʒ/ and /y/ correctly.

CUES

1. . . . use a charge card when you shop?
2. . . . jog in the morning?
3. . . . wear jeans?
4. . . . talk to strangers?
5. . . . enjoy listening to jazz?
6. . . . eat junk food?

SPELLING

FIGURE IT OUT

On page 134–135, you figured out some rules for spelling /dʒ/. Here are some words with the sounds /y/ at the beginning and in the middle. Study the spelling of these words.

/y/ *at the beginning*	/y/ *in the middle*
young	beyond
year	lawyer
use	regular
united	figure
	onion
	million

What letters make the sound /y/ at the beginning of a word? Write a spelling rule.

RULE FOR /y/ AT THE BEGINNING OF WORDS

At the beginning of a word, you can spell the sound /y/ with the letter _______ or the letter ______ .

What letters make the sound /y/ in the middle of a word? Write a spelling rule.

RULE FOR /y/ IN THE MIDDLE OF WORDS

In the middle of a word, you can spell the sound /y/ with the letter ______ , the letter ______ , or the letters ______ ______ .

PARTNER 2

1b. LISTENING DISCRIMINATION AND SPEAKING. Pair Practice Words for /tʃ/ and /ʃ/.
PARTNER 2. Use this page. PARTNER 1. Turn to page 127.

DIRECTIONS: First you are the listener. Your partner will say some words. Circle the words you hear. Ask your partner to repeat any words you do not understand. Number 1 is an example.

1.	(chop)	shop	6.	chin	shin
2.	choose	shoes	7.	catch	cash
3.	watch	wash	8.	cheat	sheet
4.	cheese	she's	9.	which	wish
5.	chip	ship	10.	cheap	sheep

Now you are the speaker. Say the words to your partner. You see the consonant sound before each word. For example, you say "Number 11 is *shin*." Repeat any words your partner does not understand.

11.	/ʃ/	shin	16.	/ʃ/	cash
12.	/tʃ/	cheese	17.	/ʃ/	shop
13.	/tʃ/	which	18.	/tʃ/	watch
14.	/ʃ/	shows	19.	/ʃ/	sheet
15.	/tʃ/	cheap	20.	/tʃ/	choose

Now compare answers with your partner.

PARTNER 2

2b. LISTENING DISCRIMINATION AND SPEAKING. Pair Practice Sentences for /tʃ/ and /ʃ/.
PARTNER 2. Use this page. PARTNER 1. Turn to page 127.

DIRECTIONS: First you are the listener. Your partner will say some sentences. Circle the word you hear. Ask your partner to repeat any sentences you do not understand. Number 1 is an example.

1. The man is ____________ the car.
   a. (watching) b. washing
2. Can you spell "____________" ?
   a. cheese b. she's
3. The ball hit her ____________ .
   a. chin b. shin
4. This is a ____________ blanket.
   a. cheap b. sheep

Now you are the speaker. Say the sentences to your partner. You see the consonant sound before each sentence. Repeat any sentences your partner does not understand.

5. /ʃ/ He always SHOWS the answer.
6. /tʃ/ Please CATCH this for me.
7. /tʃ/ How do you spell "WHICH"?
8. /ʃ/ She doesn't want TWO SHOES.

Now compare answers with your partner.

PARTNER 2

4b. SPEAKING AND LISTENING. Pair Practice for /tʃ/ and /ʃ/. PARTNER 2. Use this page. PARTNER 1. Turn to page 129.

DIRECTIONS: Your partner has a page from the Monday evening TV listing. Here is a list of TV shows. Ask your partner about times and channels of shows you want to watch. Pronounce /tʃ/ and /ʃ/ correctly.

EXAMPLE:

YOU: When is A *Shot in the Dark* showing?
YOUR PARTNER: It's showing at seven o'clock.
YOU: What channel is it on?
YOUR PARTNER: It's on channel 5.

TV SHOWS

News
WHNW News and Short Reports
International News
News with Sharon Chad
Newswatch
News with Chuck Day and Betty Short

Recreation
America's National Parks

Variety
Asher and Bush Hour

Movies
Gold Rush Days
Checkmate
A Shot in the Dark
Modern Professions

Game Shows
$1,000 March for Cash
Home Shopping Club

Education
Brush Up Your English

Series
Charles in Charge
Changing Times
Too Much, Too Soon
Cheer Up

Documentary
A Talk with the Nation

Now here is a page from the Tuesday evening TV listing.

DIRECTIONS: Your partner will ask you about the shows, show times, and channels. Use the TV listing to answer. Pronounce /tʃ/ and /ʃ/ correctly.

EXAMPLE:

YOUR PARTNER: When is *Scotch on the Rocks* showing?
YOU: It's showing at eight o'clock.
YOUR PARTNER: What channel is it on?
YOU: It's on channel 11.

TV LISTING - SHOWS FOR THIS WEEK - TUESDAY

Time	Channel	Show	Time	Channel	Show
6:00 PM	2	News with Chapman and Shumaker	8:00 PM	7	Catch the Stars
	4	WHNW News Evening Edition		11	Movie: *Scotch on the Rocks*
	7	Change in Chinatown	8:30 PM	2	Movie: *Out of Touch*
7:00 PM	2	Spin for Fortune		6	Nature
	4	The Sheriff		40	Get Rich Quick
	9	Adventure on the Ocean	9:00 PM	5	Movie: *Checkmate*
7:30 PM	4	The Shawnie Rich Show		7	On the Shelf
	7	Shootout		52	National News and Sports
	13	Movie: *Teach Me Tonight*	10:00 PM	2	News with Chester and Shipp
				13	Movie: *Picture It*

PARTNER 2

1b. SPEAKING AND LISTENING. Pair Practice for /tʃ/ and /dʒ/. PARTNER 2. Use this page. PARTNER 1. Turn to page 133.

DIRECTIONS: Here is a college schedule with information about classes. You need to know what time and where the classes meet. Take turns with your partner asking and answering questions. Pronounce /tʃ/ and /dʒ/ correctly. Write the answers on the schedule.

EXAMPLE:

YOU:	When does Geography meet?
YOUR PARTNER:	It meets Mondays, Tuesdays, Wednesdays, and Thursdays from 9 to 10.
YOU:	Where does it meet?
YOUR PARTNER:	In Lecture Hall 101.

SCHEDULE OF CLASSES - CHAMBERLAIN COLLEGE

Class	Day	Time	Room/Building
Biology	______	______	______
Engineering I	M. W.	3–5	20 Engineering
ESL: American Culture	______	______	______
ESL: Vocabulary Enrichment	W. F.	8–9:30	321 Chadwick
Geography	***M. T. W. T.***	***9–10***	***101 Lecture Hall***
Geology	Tu. Th.	11–2	B–7 Chaney Hall
Gymnastics	______	______	______
Journalism	M. T. W. T.	12–1	12 Chadwick
Management	______	______	______
Physical Education	______	______	______
Psychology I	______	______	______
Sociology	M. W. F.	9–10:30	300 St. Charles
Speech Communication	______	______	______

Now compare answers with your partner.

PARTNER 2

1b. SPEAKING AND LISTENING. Pair Practice for /dʒ/ and /y/. PARTNER 2. Use this page. PARTNER 1. Turn to page 136.

DIRECTIONS: Here is information about some presidents of the United States. Take turns asking and answering questions. Write the answers in the chart.

EXAMPLE:

YOU: When was James Monroe president of the United States?
YOUR PARTNER: James Monroe was president from 1817 to 1825.

SOME PRESIDENTS OF THE UNITED STATES

President	From	To	President	From	To
Andrew Jackson	______	______	George Bush	______	______
Jimmy Carter	1977	1980	John F. Kennedy	1961	1963
Benjamin Harrison	______	______	Lyndon Johnson	1963	1969
Thomas Jefferson	1801	1809	Gerald Ford	______	______
Ulysses S. Grant	______	______	James Monroe	*1817*	*1825*
George Washington	1789	1797	John Adams	1797	1801

Now compare answers with your partner.

LESSON 13 The Consonants /b/, /v/, /p/, and /f/

PART ONE /b/ and /v/

In English, you find the consonant sound /b/ at the beginning of a word or in the middle of a word. Not many words have /b/ at the end.

Beginning	*Middle*	*End*
big	baby	job
book	table	cab
build	about	tube
busy	public	club

You also find the consonant sound /v/ at the beginning of a word, in the middle of a word, or at the end of a word.

Beginning	*Middle*	*End*
visit	over	have
very	never	give
verb	movie	leave
vacation	travel	move

Contrasting the Consonants /b/ and /v/

WARM-UP

Look at the pictures. Listen to the words and repeat them.

1. boat /b/

2. vote /v/

ARTICULATION

Look at the pictures. The heads show how to make the sounds.

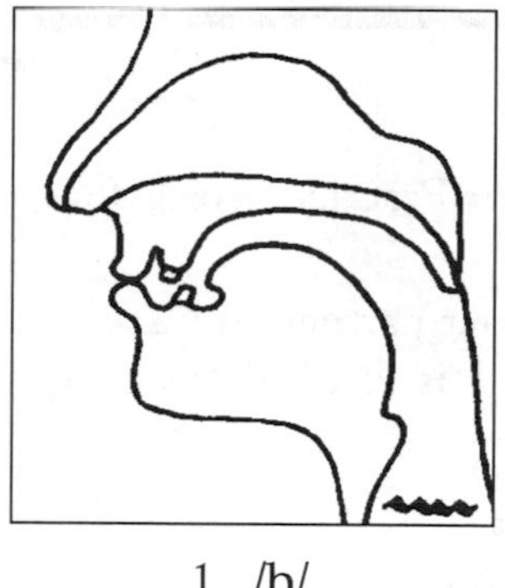

1. /b/

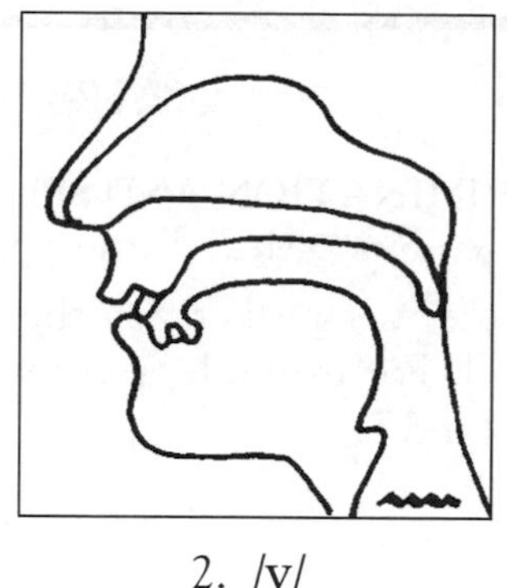

2. /v/

How are the heads the same? How are the heads different?

CONTRAST

Look at the pairs of words. Listen and repeat.

ban – van

B – V

best – vest

berry – very

LISTENING

Some words in English have the contrast between /b/ and /v/. Look again at the *boat* and *vote* pictures on page 142. /b/ is *number 1.* /v/ is *number 2.* Listen to the following words. If you hear /b/ as in *boat*, say "one." If you hear /v/ as in *vote*, say "two."

INTENSIVE PRACTICE

As a class, listen to and repeat the pairs of /b/ and /v/ words you hear.

PRONOUNCE WORDS

Listen to and repeat the /b/ words you hear. Then listen to and repeat the /v/ words you hear.

PRONOUNCE PHRASES

Listen to and repeat the phrases you hear.

PRONOUNCE SENTENCES

Listen to and repeat the sentences you hear.

PRACTICE ACTIVITIES

PARTNER 1

1a. LISTENING DISCRIMINATION AND SPEAKING. Pair Practice Words for /b/ and /v/.
PARTNER 1. Use this page. PARTNER 2. Turn to page 153.

DIRECTIONS: First you are the speaker. Say the words to your partner. You see the consonant sound before each word. For example, you say "Number 1 is *vest*." Repeat any words your partner does not understand.

1. /v/ vest
2. /b/ base
3. /b/ bet
4. /v/ curve
5. /b/ B
6. /v/ vote
7. /v/ very
8. /b/ ban

Now you are the listener. Your partner will say some words. Circle the words you hear. Ask your partner to repeat any words you do not understand. Number 9 is an example.

9. (berry) very
10. ban van
11. boat vote
12. B V
13. bet vet
14. best vest
15. base vase
16. bend vend

Now compare answers with your partner.

PARTNER 1

2a. LISTENING DISCRIMINATION AND SPEAKING. Pair Practice Sentences for /b/ and /v/. PARTNER 1. Use this page. PARTNER 2. Turn to page 153.

DIRECTIONS: First you are the speaker. Say the sentences to your partner. You see the consonant sound before each sentence. Repeat any sentences your partner does not understand.

1. /v/ I found a VASE for the flowers.
2. /b/ I will need your BOAT.
3. /b/ The car is parked on the CURB.
4. /v/ They told me about the VAN.

Now you are the listener. Your partner will say some sentences. Circle the word you hear. Ask your partner to repeat any sentences you do not understand. Number 5 is an example.

5. He talked about the __________ .
   a. (bet) b. vet
6. She's wearing her __________ .
   a. best b. vest
7. Show me the __________ .
   a. cabs b. calves
8. How many "r"s are there in "__________"?
   a. berry b. very

Now compare answers with your partner.

3. SPEAKING. Pair or Group Practice for /b/ and /v/.

DIRECTIONS: Here is a picture of a kitchen. You can see a list of things in the kitchen and a list of prepositions. Take turns asking and answering questions about the kitchen things.

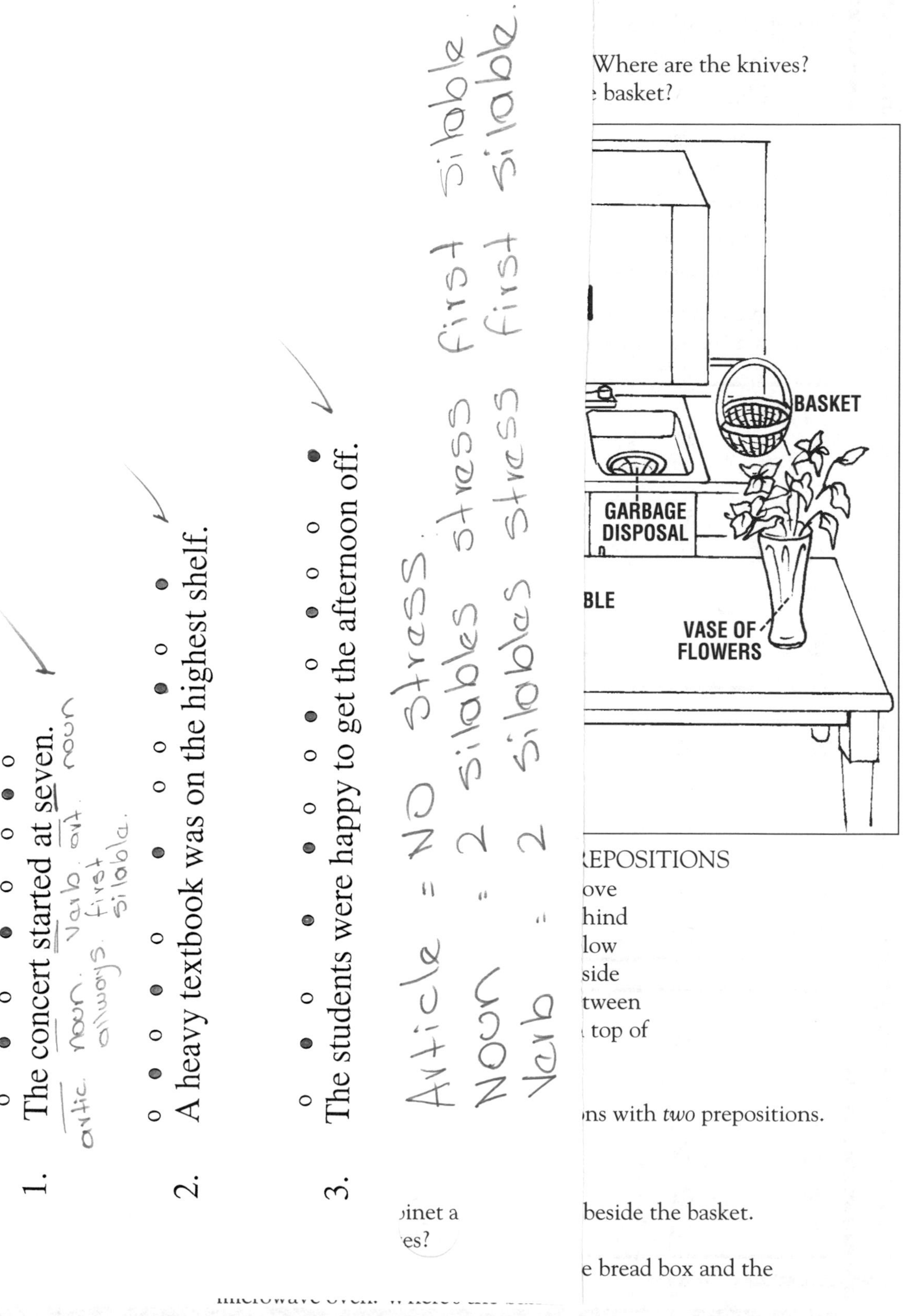

Practice Word Stress and Sentence Stress Quiz!
1. The concert started at seven.
2. A heavy textbook was on the highest shelf.
3. The students were happy to get the afternoon off.
BASKET
GARBAGE DISPOSAL
BLE
VASE OF FLOWERS

Where are the knives?

basket?

REPOSITIONS

ove

hind

low

side

tween

top of

ns with *two* prepositions.

inet a

es?

beside the basket.

e bread box and the

PARTNER 1

4a. LISTENING DISCRIMINATION AND SPEAKING. Pair Practice for /b/ and /v/.

PARTNER 1. Use this page. PARTNER 2. Turn to page 154.

DIRECTIONS: Ask your partner about the dates of these holidays. Write the dates on the lines.

EXAMPLE:

When is Valentine's Day? *February 14*

1. . . . Labor Day? ______________________
2. . . . Washington's Birthday? ______________________
3. . . . Lincoln's Birthday? ______________________
4. . . . Grandparents' Day? ______________________
5. . . . Presidents' Day? ______________________

Here are calendars for October, November, and December. Listen to your partner and tell the months and days of the holidays. Ask your partner to repeat any questions you do not understand.

OCTOBER

S	M	T	W	T	F	S
				1	2	3
4	5	6	7	8	9	10
11	12 Columbus Day	13	14	15	16	17
18	19	20	21	22	23	24
25	26	27	28	29	30	31

NOVEMBER

S	M	T	W	T	F	S
1	2	3 Election Day	4	5	6	7
8	9	10	11 Veterans Day	12	13	14
15	16	17	18	19	20	21
22	23	24	25	26 Thanksgiving Day	27	28
29	30					

DECEMBER

S	M	T	W	T	F	S
		1	2	3	4	5
6	7	8	9	10	11	12
13	15	15	16	17	18	19
20	21	22	23	24	25 Christmas	26
27	28	29	30	31 New Year's Eve		

SPELLING

FIGURE IT OUT

Here are some words with the sound /b/. You can see some words with the sound /v/, too. Study the spelling of these words.

/b/			/v/		
book	absent	verb	voice	travel	five
build	hobby	robe	verb	every	have
double	rabbit		vowel	invite	leave

What letters make the sounds /b/ and /v/? How many letters make the sounds /b/ and /v/ in the middle of a word? What about "e" at the end of a word? Write a spelling rule for each sound.

RULES

1. Say the sound /b/ when a word is spelled with the consonant letter ________ . In the middle of a word, you can find ______ or ______ consonant letters for the sound /b/. The letter *e* at the end of a word is *(circle one)* pronounced not pronounced.

There are a few exceptions to Rule 1. Your instructor will pronounce the following list of words. Listen carefully to these words.

thumb, comb, doubt

How did your instructor pronounce *b* in these words?

2. Say the sound /v/ when a word is spelled with the consonant letter ________ . Spell the sound /v/ with ________ consonant letter. The letter *e* at the end of a word is *(circle one)* pronounced not pronounced.

There is one exception to Rule 2. Your instructor will pronounce the following word. Listen carefully to it.

of

PART TWO /p/ and /f/

In English, you find the consonant sound /p/ at the beginning of a word, in the middle of a word, or at the end of a word.

Beginning	*Middle*	*End*
pass	happy	keep
pay	open	stop
put	paper	trip
play	people	up

You also find the consonant sound /f/ at the beginning of a word, in the middle of a word, or at the end of a word.

Beginning	*Middle*	*End*
find	after	safe
fall	coffee	wife
phone	traffic	laugh
fast	careful	belief

Contrasting the Consonants /p/ and /f/

WARM-UP

Look at the pictures. Listen to the words and repeat them.

1. pan /p/

2. fan /f/

ARTICULATION

Look at the pictures. The heads show how to make the sounds.

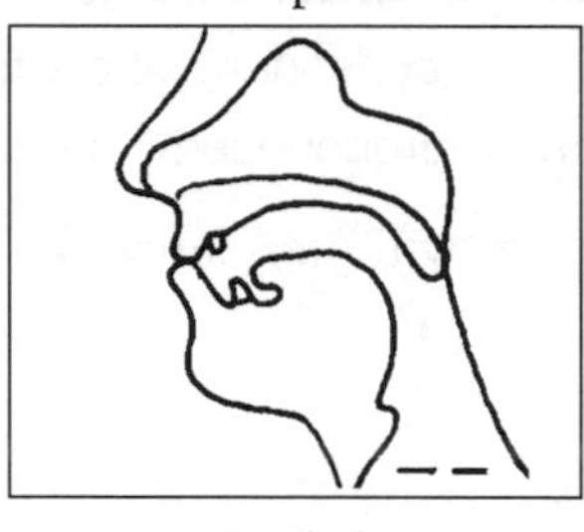

1. /p/

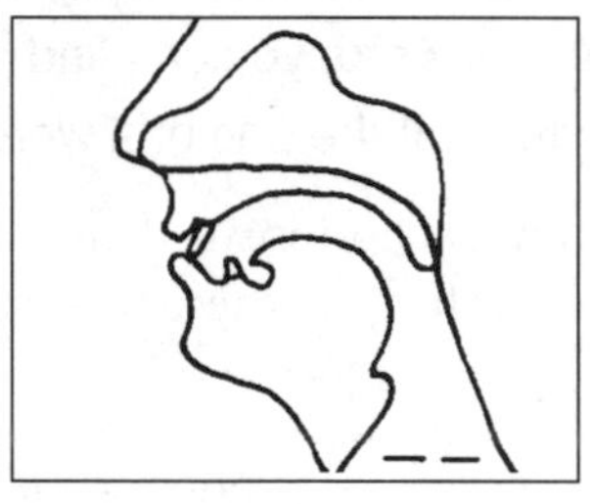

2. /f/

How are the heads the same? How are the heads different?

CONTRAST

Look at the pairs of words. Listen and repeat.

pig – fig   leap – leaf   cup – cuff   past – fast

/p/ AT THE BEGINNING OF A WORD

To clearly pronounce /p/ at the beginning of a word, push the air from your lips. Put your hand in front of your mouth. Say /p/. You can feel the air. Listen to this example:

pat, pat, pat

Now repeat the words with /p/ at the beginning. Push the air from your lips when you say /p/.

pack   pig   pie   pound   pea   push

LISTENING

Some words in English have the contrast between /p/ and /f/. Look again at the *pan* and *fan* pictures above. /p/ is *number 1*. /f/ is *number 2*. Listen to the following words. If you hear /p/ as in *pan*, say "one." If you hear /f/ as in *fan*, say "two."

INTENSIVE PRACTICE

As a class, listen to and repeat the pairs of /p/ and /f/ words you hear.

PRONOUNCE WORDS

Listen to and repeat the /p/ words you hear. Then listen to and repeat the /f/ words you hear.

PRONOUNCE PHRASES

Listen to and repeat the phrases you hear.

PRONOUNCE SENTENCES

Listen to and repeat the sentences you hear.

PRACTICE ACTIVITIES

PARTNER 1

1a. LISTENING DISCRIMINATION AND SPEAKING. Pair Practice Words for /p/ and /f/.
PARTNER 1. Use this page. PARTNER 2. Turn to page 155.

DIRECTIONS: First you are the speaker. Say the words to your partner. You see the consonant sound before each word. For example, you say "Number 1 is *fat*." Repeat any words your partner does not understand.

1. /f/ fat
2. /p/ cheap
3. /p/ pace
4. /f/ fool
5. /f/ fair
6. /f/ fan
7. /f/ wife
8. /f/ fit

Now you are the listener. Your partner will say some words. Circle the words you hear. Ask your partner to repeat any words you do not understand. Number 9 is an example.

9. leap (leaf)
10. pin fin
11. pork fork
12. cup cuff
13. past fast
14. pig fig
15. pat fat
16. pace face

Now compare answers with your partner.

PARTNER 1

2a. LISTENING DISCRIMINATION AND SPEAKING. Pair Practice Sentences for /p/ and /f/.
PARTNER 1. Use this page. PARTNER 2. Turn to page 155.

DIRECTIONS: First you are the speaker. Say the sentences to your partner. You see the consonant sound before each sentence. Repeat any sentences your partner does not understand.

1. /f/ We like his FACE.
2. /p/ The PAN is in the kitchen.
3. /f/ Your CUFF is dirty.
4. /p/ It's a PAIR game.

Now you are the listener. Your partner will say some sentences. Circle the word you hear. Ask your partner to repeat any sentences you do not understand. Number 5 is an example.

5. What's this ____________ ?
   a. pore b. (for)
6. ____________ this fruit.
   a. Peel b. Feel
7. Do you want the ____________ ?
   a. pork b. fork
8. It's a ______________ story.
   a. past b. fast

Now compare answers with your partner.

3. SPEAKING. Guided Conversation to Practice /p/ and /f/.

DIRECTIONS: Imagine you are at a supermarket. Here is a shopping list. Here is a list of departments in the supermarket, too. Take turns being the shopper and the clerk. Clearly pronounce the difference between /p/ and /f/.

EXAMPLE:

SHOPPER: Excuse me. Do you know where I can pick up some coffee filters?
CLERK: You'll find that in the Paper Goods Department.
SHOPPER: Thanks.
CLERK: You're welcome.

SHOPPING LIST		DEPARTMENTS
some pork	some potatoes	Produce
some grapes	some paper towels	Fish
some shrimp	some cough drops	Meat
a pound of dog food	some cat food	Pharmacy
some beef	a pineapple	Pet Food
some coffee filters	some pain pills	Paper Goods
some aspirin	some green peppers	
a pound of fish		

MODEL CONVERSATION

SHOPPER: Excuse me. Do you know where I can pick up ______________________________?
CLERK: You'll find that in the ____________________ Department.
SHOPPER: Thanks.
CLERK: You're welcome.

4. SPEAKING. Pair or Group Practice for /p/ and /f/.

DIRECTIONS: On page 151 is a picture of an office. You can see a list of things in the office and a list of prepositions. Take turns asking and answering questions about the office things. Use prepositions from the list.

EXAMPLE:

STUDENT 1: Where's the stapler?
STUDENT 2: It's on top of the photocopy machine. Where are the paper clips?
STUDENT 3: They're to the right of the pair of scissors. Where's the folder?

OFFICE THINGS		PREPOSITIONS
a file cabinet	paper clips	above
a wastepaper basket	a stapler	on top of
a folder	a pair of scissors	in front of
a typewriter	a phone	to the left of
a word processor	a photocopy machine	to the right of
a fax machine	a coffee machine	between
a tape dispenser		

****Challenge!** Now ask questions again. Answer the questions with *two* prepositions.

EXAMPLE:

STUDENT 1: Where's the stapler?
STUDENT 2: It's on top of the photocopy machine to the right of the fax machine. Where are the paper clips?
STUDENT 3: They're to the right of the pair of scissors above the wastepaper basket. Where's the folder?

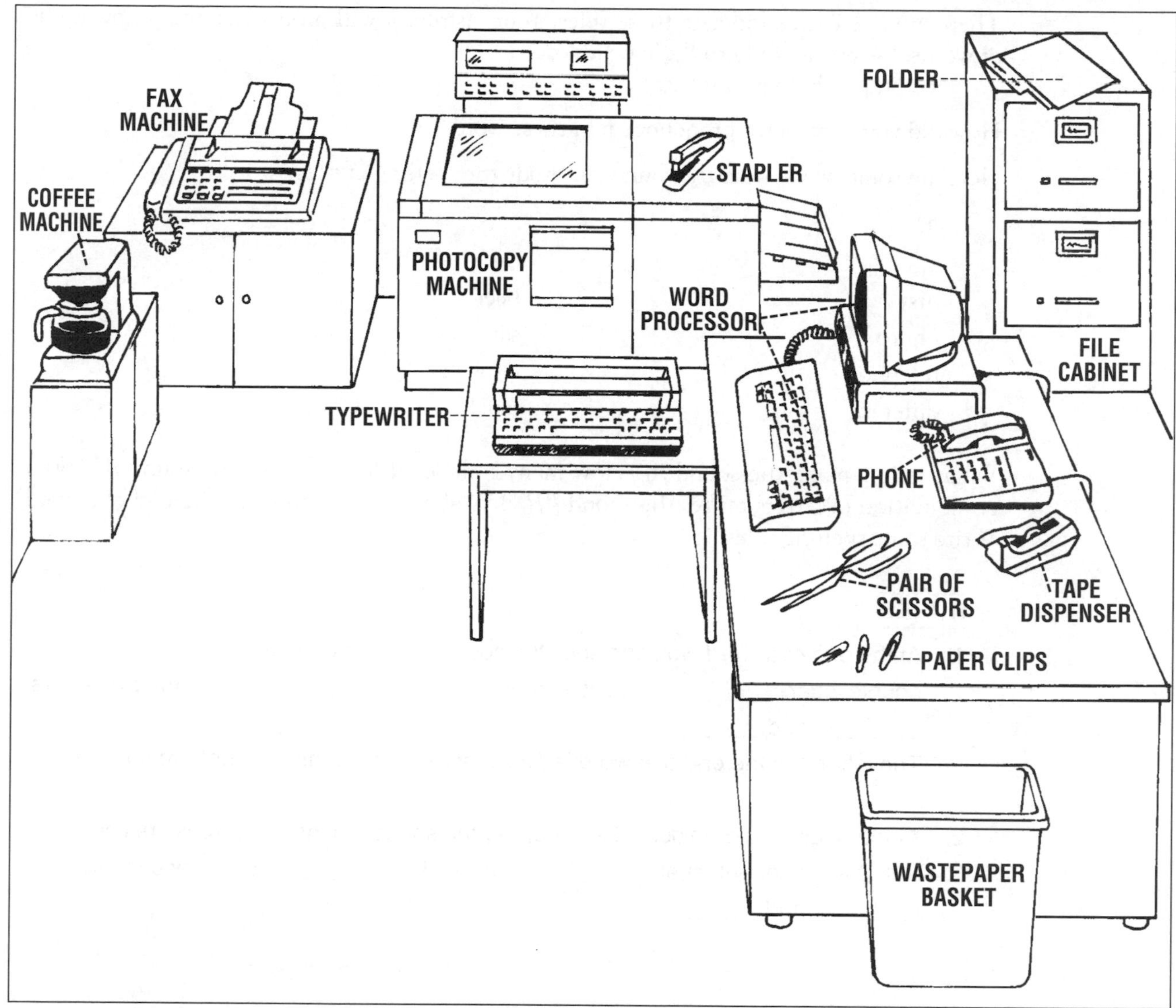

SPELLING

FIGURE IT OUT

Here are some words with the sound /p/. Study the spelling of these words.

/p/	
put	happy
pencil	stopping
purple	up
rapid	hope

What letter makes the sound /p/? How many letters make the sound /p/ in the middle of a word? What about *e* at the end of a word? Write a spelling rule.

RULE

Say the sound /p/ when a word is spelled with the consonant letter _______ . In the middle of a word, you can find _______ or _______ consonant letters for the sound /p/. The letter *e* at the end of a word is *(circle one)* pronounced not pronounced.

There are a few exceptions to these rules. Your instructor will pronounce the following list of words. Listen carefully to these words.

receipt, psychology, raspberry

How did your instructor pronounce *p* in these words?

Here are some words with the sound /f/. Study the spelling of these words.

/f/	
fall	off
first	beef
photo	safe
telephone	enough
different	laugh

What letters make the sound /f/? How many individual letters make the sound /f/? What combination of letters makes the sound /f/? How about the sound /f/ at the end of a word? Write some spelling rules.

RULES

1. At the end of a word, you can spell the sound /f/ with the letter ________ , double letter ________ , the two letters ________ and ________ , or the two letters ________ and ________ .

   The letter *e* at the end of a word is *(circle one)* pronounced not pronounced.

2. At the beginning or middle of a word, say the sound /f/ when a word is spelled with the consonant letter ________ , double letter ________ , or the two letters ________ and ________ .

PARTNER 2

1b. LISTENING DISCRIMINATION AND SPEAKING. Pair Practice Words for /b/ and /v/.
PARTNER 2. Use this page. PARTNER 1. Turn to page 144.

DIRECTIONS: First you are the listener. Your partner will say some words. Circle the words you hear. Ask your partner to repeat any words you do not understand. Number 1 is an example.

1. best (vest)
2. base vase
3. bet vet
4. curb curve
5. B V
6. boat vote
7. berry very
8. ban van

Now you are the speaker. Say the words to your partner. You see the consonant sound before each word. For example, you say "Number 9 is *berry*." Repeat any words your partner does not understand.

9. /b/ berry
10. /v/ van
11. /b/ boat
12. /v/ V
13. /b/ bet
14. /v/ vest
15. /v/ vase
16. /v/ vend

Now compare answers with your partner.

PARTNER 2

2b. LISTENING DISCRIMINATION AND SPEAKING. Pair Practice Sentences for /b/ and /v/.
PARTNER 2. Use this page. PARTNER 1. Turn to page 144.

DIRECTIONS: First you are the listener. Your partner will say some sentences. Circle the word you hear. Ask your partner to repeat any sentences you do not understand. Number 1 is an example.

1. I found a ____________ for the flowers.
   a. base b. (vase)
2. I will need your ______________ .
   a. boat b. vote
3. The car is parked on the ____________ .
   a. curb b. curve
4. They told me about the ____________ .
   a. ban b. van

Now you are the speaker. Say the sentences to your partner. You see the consonant sound before each sentence. Repeat any sentences your partner does not understand.

5. /b/ He talked about the BET.
6. /v/ She's wearing her VEST.
7. /b/ Show me the CABS.
8. /v/ How many "r"s are there in "VERY"?

Now compare answers with your partner.

PARTNER 2

4b. LISTENING DISCRIMINATION AND SPEAKING. Pair Practice for /b/ and /v/.
PARTNER 2. Use this page. PARTNER 1. Turn to page 146.

DIRECTIONS: Here are calendars for February and September. Listen to your partner and tell the months and days of the holidays. Ask your partner to repeat any questions you do not understand.

FEBRUARY

S	M	T	W	T	F	S
						1
2	3	4	5	6	7	8
9	10	11	12 Lincoln's Birthday	13	14 Valentine's Day	15
16	17 Presidents' Day	18	19	20	21	22 Washington's Birthday
23	24	25	26	27	28	29

SEPTEMBER

S	M	T	W	T	F	S
		1	2	3	4	5
6	7 Labor Day	8	9	10	11	12
13 Grandparents' Day	14	15	16	17	18	19
20	21	22	23	24	25	26
27	28	29	30			

Now ask your partner about the dates of these holidays. Write the dates on the lines.

EXAMPLE:
When is Election Day? ***November 3***

6. . . . Thanksgiving? ______________________
7 . . . Columbus Day? ______________________
8. . . . Veterans Day? ______________________
9. . . . New Year's Eve? ______________________
10. . . . Christmas? ______________________

PARTNER 2

1b. LISTENING DISCRIMINATION AND SPEAKING. Pair Practice Words for /p/ and /f/.
PARTNER 2. Use this page. PARTNER 1. Turn to page 149.

DIRECTIONS: First you are the listener. Your partner will say some words. Circle the words you hear. Ask your partner to repeat any words you do not understand. Number 1 is an example.

1. pat (fat)
2. cheap chief
3. pace face
4. pool fool
5. pair fair
6. pan fan
7. wipe wife
8. pit fit

Now you are the speaker. Say the words to your partner. You see the consonant sound before each word. For example, you say "Number 9 is *leaf*." Repeat any words your partner does not understand.

9. /f/ leaf
10. /p/ pin
11. /f/ fork
12. /p/ cup
13. /f/ fast
14. /p/ pig
15. /f/ fat
16. /f/ face

Now compare answers with your partner.

PARTNER 2

2b. LISTENING DISCRIMINATION AND SPEAKING. Pair Practice Sentences for /p/ and /f/.
PARTNER 2. Use this page. PARTNER 1. Turn to page 149.

DIRECTIONS: First you are the listener. Your partner will say some sentences. Circle the word you hear. Ask your partner to repeat any sentences you do not understand. Number 1 is an example.

1. We like his ____________ .
   a. pace b. (face)
2. The ____________ is in the kitchen.
   a. pan b. fan
3. Your ____________ is dirty.
   a. cup b. cuff
4. It's a ____________ game.
   a. pair b. fair

Now you are the speaker. Say the sentences to your partner. You see the consonant sound before each sentence. Repeat any sentences your partner does not understand.

5. /f/ What's this FOR?
6. /p/ PEEL this fruit.
7. /f/ Do you want the FORK?
8. /f/ It's a FAST story.

Now compare answers with your partner.

LESSON **14**

The Consonants /l/ and /r/

PART ONE /l/ and /r/

In English, you find the consonant sound /l/ at the beginning of a word, in the middle of a word, or at the end of a word.

Beginning	*Middle*	*End*
low	below	all
live	only	sell
laugh	pilot	smile
look	English	hotel

You find the consonant sound /r/ at the beginning of a word, in the middle of a word, or at the end of a word, too.

Beginning	*Middle*	*End*
red	art	car
room	work	hair
ride	person	after
run	morning	paper

Contrasting the Consonants /l/ and /r/

WARM-UP

Look at the pictures. Listen to the words and repeat them.

1. lock /l/

2. rock /r/

ARTICULATION

Look at the pictures. The heads show how to make the sounds.

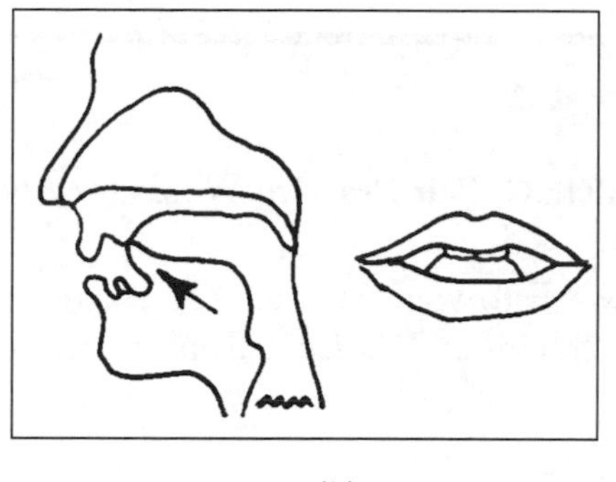

1. /l/

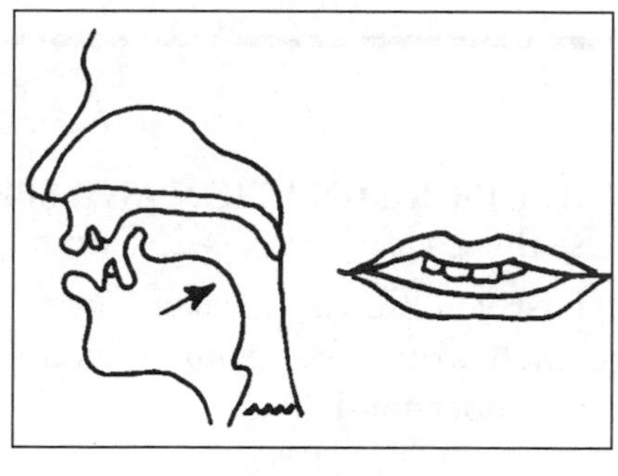

2. /r/

How are the heads the same? How are the heads and lips different?

CONTRAST

Look at the pairs of words. Listen and repeat.

lace – race

long – wrong

lake – rake

light – right

LISTENING

Many words in English have the contrast between /l/ and /r/. Look again at the *lock* and *rock* pictures on page 156. /l/ is *number 1.* /r/ is *number 2.* Listen to the following words. If you hear /l/ as in *lock*, say "one." If you hear /r/ as in *rock*, say "two."

INTENSIVE PRACTICE

As a class, listen to and repeat the pairs of /l/ and /r/ words you hear.

PRONOUNCE WORDS

Listen to and repeat the /l/ words you hear. Then listen to and repeat the /r/ words you hear.

PRONOUNCE PHRASES

Listen to and repeat the phrases you hear.

PRONOUNCE SENTENCES

Listen to and repeat the sentences you hear.

PRACTICE ACTIVITIES

PARTNER 1

1a. LISTENING DISCRIMINATION AND SPEAKING. Pair Practice Words for /l/ and /r/.
PARTNER 1. Use this page. PARTNER 2. Turn to page 168.

DIRECTIONS: First you are the speaker. Say the words to your partner. You see the consonant sound before each word. For example, you say "Number 1 is *led*." Repeat any words your partner does not understand.

1. /l/ led
2. /l/ low
3. /r/ rake
4. /l/ lip
5. /r/ road
6. /r/ right
7. /r/ wrong
8. /l/ alive

Now you are the listener. Your partner will say some words. Circle the words you hear. Ask your partner to repeat any words you do not understand. Number 9 is an example.

9. (lace) race
10. collect correct
11. low row
12. light right
13. lock rock
14. led red
15. long wrong
16. lake rake

Now compare answers with your partner.

PARTNER 1

2a. LISTENING DISCRIMINATION AND SPEAKING. Pair Practice Sentences for /l/ and /r/. PARTNER 1. Use this page. PARTNER 2. Turn to page 168.

DIRECTIONS: First you are the speaker. Say the sentences to your partner. You see the consonant sound before each sentence. Repeat any sentences your partner does not understand.

1. /r/ This ROCK is heavy.
2. /l/ She has a LONG number.
3. /r/ It's a picture of the RACE.
4. /l/ He sat by the LAKE.

Now you are the listener. Your partner will say some sentences. Circle the word you hear. Ask your partner to repeat any sentences you do not understand. Number 5 is an example.

5. ____________ the homework.
   a. (Collect) b. Correct
6. Do you have the ____________ one?
   a. light b. right
7. I can't break this ____________.
   a. lock b. rock
8. Put this on your ____________.
   a. list b. wrist

Now compare answers with your partner.

3. SPEAKING. Pair or Group Practice for /l/ and /r/. Here are some road signs and their meanings.

DIRECTIONS: Take turns asking and answering questions about the road signs. Use the list of meanings.

EXAMPLE:

STUDENT 1: What does number three mean?
STUDENT 2: It means "Road Narrows." What does number eleven mean?
STUDENT 3: It means "No Left Turn." What does . . .

1

2

3

4

5

6

7

8

9

10

11

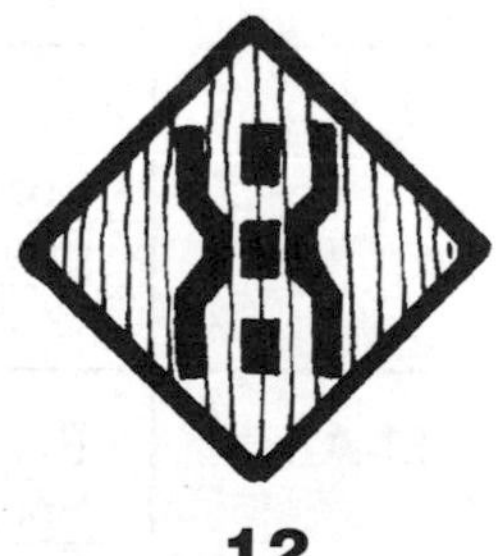

12

ROAD SIGNS

Crossroad
Fire Station
Hill
Keep Left
Left Turn Only
Narrow Bridge
No Left Turn
No Parking
Railroad Crossing
Right Turn Only
Road Narrows
Speed Limit

PARTNER 1

4a. SPEAKING AND LISTENING. Pair Practice for /l/ and /r/. PARTNER 1. Use this page. PARTNER 2. Turn to page 169.

DIRECTIONS: Here are results of an English test for different students. Your partner has some English test results, too. Take turns asking and answering questions. Make an X on the answers. Pronounce /l/ and /r/ correctly.

EXAMPLE:

YOU: How is Reza's spelling?
YOUR PARTNER: Average. How is Richard's grammar?
YOU: Very good. How is . . .

RESULTS OF ENGLISH TEST

Student	Skill	Excellent	Very Good	Average	Below Average
Reza	Reading				
	Spelling			X	
	Grammar	X			
	Pronunciation			X	
Helga	Reading				X
	Spelling				
	Grammar		X		
	Pronunciation				
Richard	Reading				
	Spelling				X
	Grammar		X		
	Pronunciation				
Rolfe	Reading	X			
	Spelling				
	Grammar				
	Pronunciation				X
El-Ali	Reading				
	Spelling				X
	Grammar				
	Pronunciation		X		
Lenore	Reading				
	Spelling				
	Grammar	X			
	Pronunciation		X		

Now compare answers with your partner.

PARTNER 1

5a. SPEAKING AND LISTENING. Where in the World? Pair Practice for /l/ and /r/.
PARTNER 1. Use this page. PARTNER 2. Turn to page 170.

DIRECTIONS: Ask your partner where in the world the cities are. Repeat any questions your partner does not understand. If your partner does not know the answer, tell your partner the answer.

EXAMPLE:

YOU: Where in the world is Lima?
YOUR PARTNER: Lima is in Peru.

1. . . . London? (England)
2. . . . Istanbul? (Turkey)
3. . . . Calcutta? (India)
4. . . . St. Petersburg? (Russia)
5. . . . Cairo? (Egypt)
6. . . . Berlin? (Germany)

Now your partner will ask you where some cities are. Answer with the country. Ask your partner to repeat any questions you do not understand. Your partner will tell you the answer if you do not know.

EXAMPLE:

YOUR PARTNER: Where in the world is Lima?
YOU: Lima is in Peru.

6. READ AND REPORT. Your Personality in the Stars. Group or Class Activity to Practice /l/ and /r/. The place of the stars and planets in the sky gives us our horoscope. A horoscope tells you about your personality. You find information if you look for your birthday.

DIRECTIONS: First, find your birthday on page 162. Read the horoscope for your birthday. Next, tell the other students in your class or group about your horoscope. Is your horoscope true for *you?*

EXAMPLE:

"I'm an Aquarius. Part of my horoscope is true for me. An Aquarius is friendly and curious. Curious means you want to know about everything. I'm curious and friendly. An Aquarius is creative. I'm creative. I like to draw pictures and sing songs. The lucky number is 8. 8 is a lucky number for me.

Part of my horoscope is not true for me. An Aquarius is very different from most people. I'm not different from most people. I am traditional. An Aquarius likes to be with a Leo. I don't know a lot of Leo people. I have a lot of Cancer friends."

HOROSCOPES - YOUR PERSONALITY IN THE STARS

Aquarius Jan. 20 – Feb. 18
An Aquarius is friendly and curious. He/She wants to know about everything. The Aquarius personality is unusual and different. He/She is also creative. An Aquarius can understand other people very well. Other people can easily hurt an Aquarius' feelings. Lucky Number: 8. Best Friends: Leo.

Pisces Feb. 19 – Mar. 20
A Pisces is polite and patient. He/She likes to think about things that are not material. A Pisces does not have traditional ideas. He/She also likes a challenge. Lucky Numbers: 5, 9. Best Friends: Virgo.

Aries Mar. 21 – Apr. 19
An Aries has a lot of energy. He/She likes to do things without help from others. An Aries sometimes does not plan before doing something. He/She also loves change. An Aries is happy if people encourage him/her. Lucky Number: 3. Best Friends: Libra.

Taurus Apr. 20 – May 20
A Taurus is practical. He/She does not often talk about him/herself or give opinions. A Taurus wants to reach a goal and does not stop. He/She is a true friend. A Taurus is happy if other people are also true friends. Lucky Number: 7. Best Friends: Scorpio.

Gemini May 21 – June 20
A Gemini is full of charm. He/She likes material things. A Gemini is also able to do many things. It is easy for a Gemini to show the good parts of his/her personality. Other people can easily hurt a Gemini's feelings. Lucky Number: 4. Best Friends: Sagittarius.

Cancer June 21 – July 22
A Cancer has a strong imagination. He/She loves family life. A Cancer understands other people well. He/She also has a good memory. A Cancer always tries his/her best. Lucky Number: 2. Best Friends: Capricorn.

Leo July 23 – Aug. 22
A Leo is very proud. He/She likes to be with other people. It is difficult for other people to hurt a Leo. He/She also loves life. A Leo is a born leader. Lucky Number: 1. Best Friends: Aquarius.

Virgo Aug. 23 – Sept. 22
A Virgo is clever. He/She makes wise decisions. A Virgo is organized. He/She is also a true friend. A Virgo likes to plan things and then do them. He/She likes to help other people. Lucky Number: 4. Best Friends: Pisces.

Libra Sept. 23 – Oct. 22
A Libra is curious. He/She believes most people and things are good. A Libra likes to think about things and be creative. He/She is happy when life is balanced. Lucky Number: 6. Best Friends: Aries.

Scorpio Oct. 23 – Nov. 21
People enjoy being with a Scorpio. A Scorpio wants to reach a goal and does not stop. He/She is sometimes jealous. A Scorpio likes to think for a long time about things. He/She sometimes does not tell other people his/her ideas. Scorpio also loves to solve mysteries. Lucky Number: 3. Best Friends: Taurus.

Sagittarius Nov. 22 – Dec. 21
A Sagittarius loves adventure. He/She is a true friend. A Sagittarius likes to do things without help from others. He/She is always ready to work. A Sagittarius also enjoys being with friends. He/She is frank. Lucky Number: 5. Best Friends: Gemini.

Capricorn Dec. 22 – Jan. 19
A Capricorn is practical. He/She has a lot of energy. A Capricorn likes to control his/her life. He/She makes wise decisions. A Capricorn also finishes things on time. Other people usually trust a Capricorn. Lucky Number: 7. Best Friends: Cancer.

PART TWO /l/ and /r/ After Vowels

On pages 156–157, you read about the sounds /l/ and /r/ at the beginning, in the middle, and at the end of a word.

/l/ AND /r/ AFTER VOWELS

Say the vowel /ə/ *before* /l/ or /r/ to clearly pronounce /l/ or /r/. Your tongue relaxes when you say /ə/. The shape of your tongue is flat. It is easy to shape your tongue for /l/ or /r/ from the /ə/ position. Listen to these examples:

/fiy/, /əl/, /fiyəl/ (feel) /fiy/, /ər/, /fiyər/ (fear)

Now repeat the pairs of sounds and words with /l/ and /r/ after vowels.

/pey/, /əl/, /peyəl/ (pail)	/bow/, /əl/, /bowəl/ (bowl)
/pey/, /ər/, /peyər/ (pear)	/bow/, /ər/, /bowər/ (bore)
/hiy/, /əl/, /hiyəl/ (heel)	/fay/, /əl/, /fayəl/ (file)
/hiy/, /ər/, /hiyər/ (hear)	/fay/, /ər/, /fayər/ (fire)

WARM-UP

Look at the pictures. Listen to the words and repeat them.

1. pail /l/

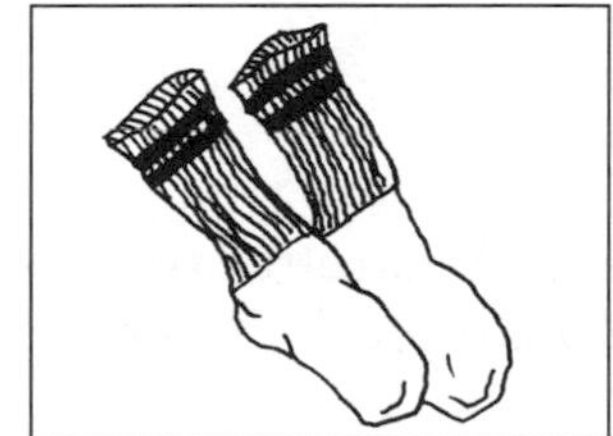

2. pair /r/

ARTICULATION

Look at the pictures. The heads show how to make the sounds.

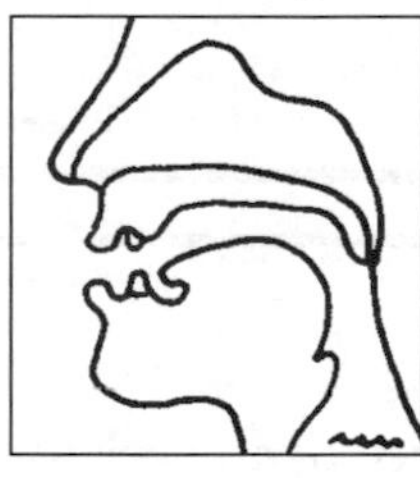

1. a. /ə/

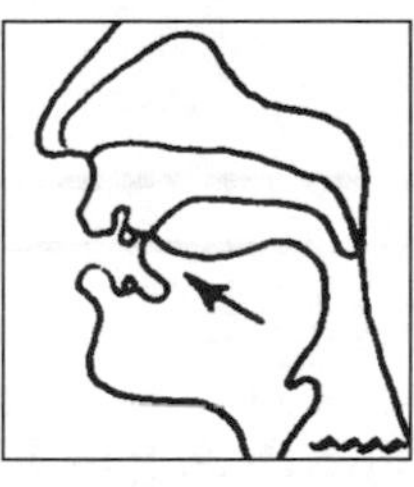

b. /l/

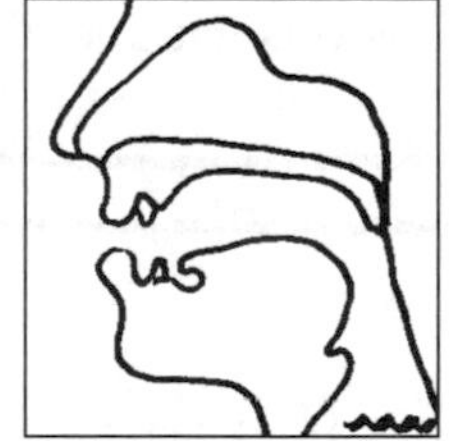

2. a. /ə/

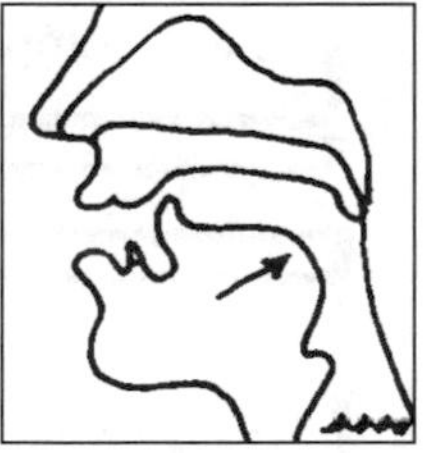

b. /r/

CONTRAST

Look at the pairs of words. Listen and repeat.

all – are   tail – tear   well – were   wheel – we're

LISTENING

Some words in English have the contrast between /l/ and /r/ after vowels. Look again at the *pail* and *pair* pictures above. /l/ is *number 1*. /r/ is *number 2*. Listen to the following words. If you hear /l/ at the end as in *pail*, say "one." If you hear /r/ at the end as in *pair*, say "two."

INTENSIVE PRACTICE

As a class, listen to and repeat the pairs of /l/ and /r/ words you hear.

PRONOUNCE WORDS

Listen to and repeat the /l/ words you hear. Then listen to and repeat the /r/ words you hear.

PRONOUNCE PHRASES

Listen to and repeat the phrases you hear.

PRONOUNCE SENTENCES

Listen to and repeat the sentences you hear.

PRACTICE ACTIVITIES

PARTNER 1

1a. LISTENING DISCRIMINATION AND SPEAKING. Pair Practice Words for /l/ and /r/ after Vowels. PARTNER 1. Use this page. PARTNER 2. Turn to page 171.

DIRECTIONS: First you are the speaker. Say the words to your partner. You see the consonant sound after each word. For example, you say "Number 1 is *are*." Repeat any words your partner does not understand.

1. are /r/
2. ball /l/
3. fear /r/
4. wheel /l/
5. fail /l/
6. wear /r/
7. tail /l/
8. tower /r/

Now you are the listener. Your partner will say some words. Circle the words you hear. Ask your partner to repeat any words you do not understand. Number 9 is an example.

9. (while) wire
10. pail pair
11. heel hear
12. fall far
13. well were
14. call car
15. fail fair
16. tail tear

Now compare answers with your partner.

PARTNER 1

2a. LISTENING DISCRIMINATION AND SPEAKING. Pair Practice Sentences for /l/ and /r/ after Vowels. PARTNER 1. Use this page. PARTNER 2. Turn to page 171.

DIRECTIONS: First you are the speaker. Say the sentences to your partner. You see the consonant sound before each sentence. Repeat any sentences your partner does not understand.

1. /r/ He got a CAR yesterday.
2. /r/ Do you know the word "WIRE"?
3. /l/ We saw a TOWEL.
4. /l/ What do you FEEL?

Now you are the listener. Your partner will say some sentences. Circle the word you hear. Ask your partner to repeat any sentences you do not understand. Number 5 is an example.

5. This coat has a ___________ .
   a. tail b. (tear)
6. She didn't say "___________ ."
   a. all b. are
7. September is___________ .
   a. fall b. far
8. You need a ___________ to play the game.
   a. ball b. bar

Now compare answers with your partner.

3. SPEAKING. Pair or Group Practice for /l/ and /r/ after Vowels. Here is a picture of shapes.

DIRECTIONS: Take turns asking and answering questions about the list of shapes. Use expressions from the list.

EXAMPLE:

STUDENT 1: Where's the triangle?
STUDENT 2: It's in the upper right corner. Where's the little circle?
STUDENT 3: It's in the lower center. Where's the oval?

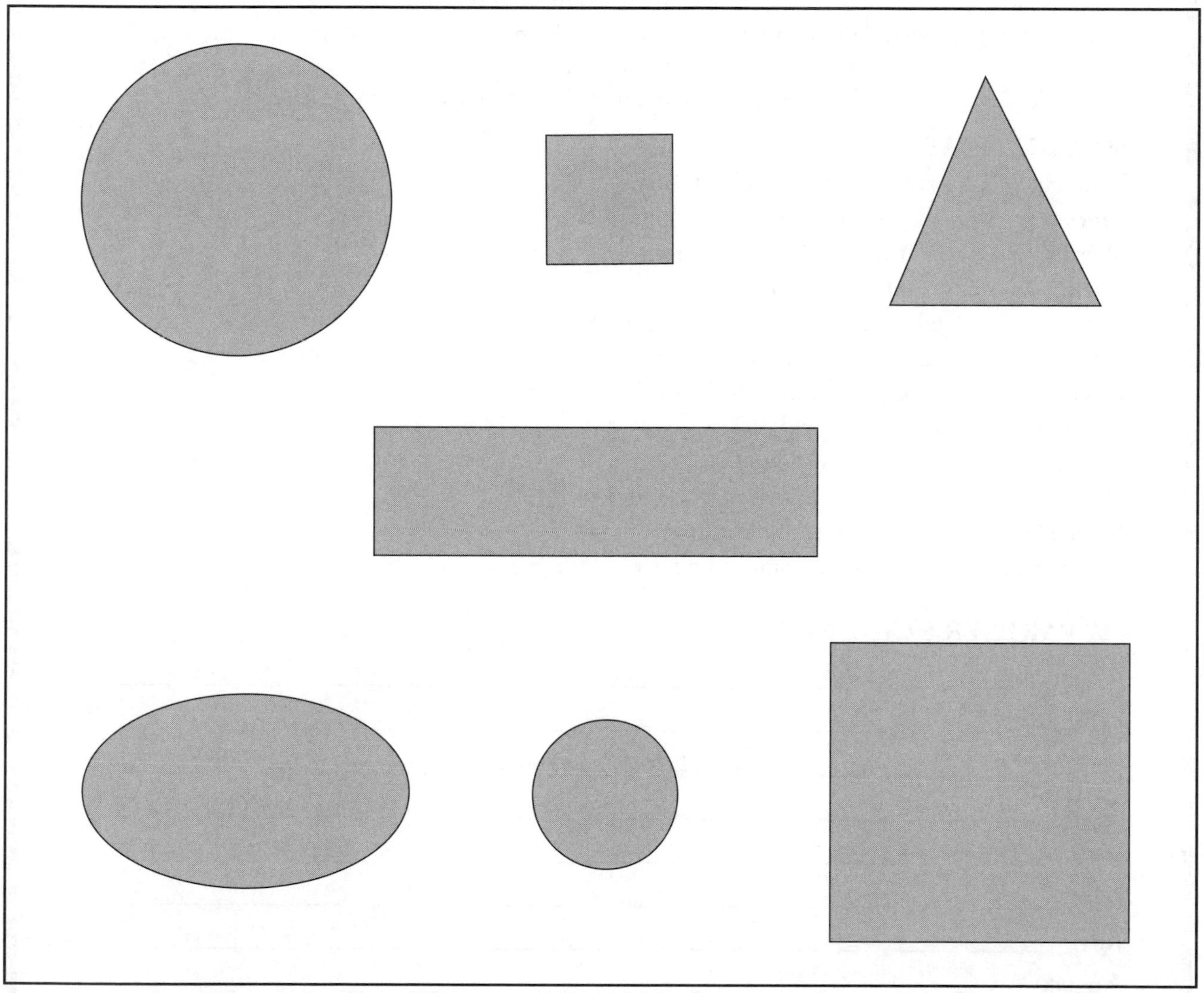

SHAPES	EXPRESSIONS
big circle	upper left corner
little circle	upper right corner
oval	upper center
rectangle	middle
big square	lower left corner
little square	lower right corner
triangle	lower center

PARTNER 1

4a. SPEAKING AND LISTENING. Pair Practice for /l/ and /r/ after Vowels. PARTNER 1. Use this page. PARTNER 2. Turn to page 172.

DIRECTIONS: You and your partner want to do some interesting things together next year. Here is your calendar. It shows some things you will do. Find out your partner's plans for next year. Take turns asking and answering questions. Pronounce /l/ and /r/ correctly.

EXAMPLE:

YOU:	What are you going to do in March?
YOUR PARTNER:	I'm going to take a class to learn about computers.
	What are you going to do in November?
YOU:	I'm going to volunteer at the library. What are you . . .

MY CALENDAR

January:	go to the opera in New York
February:	take a trip to the state capital
March:	visit my uncle in California
April:	tour Central America
May:	take a class at a technical college
June:	go to a lecture on employment
July:	take the children to Disneyland
August:	work at a local gallery
September:	travel in Europe
October:	go to a professional conference in Dallas
November:	volunteer at the library
December:	take a final exam in English

MY PARTNER'S CALENDAR

January ____________________

February ____________________

March ______ ***Take a class to learn about computers*** ______

April ____________________

May ____________________

June ____________________

July ____________________

August ____________________

September ____________________

October ____________________

November ____________________

December ____________________

What activities can you and your partner do together next year?

SPELLING

FIGURE IT OUT

Here are some words with the sounds /l/ and /r/ at the beginning. Study the spelling of these words.

/l/	/r/
look	rich
land	rose
live	run
lady	write
luck	wrist

What letters make the sounds /l/ and /r/ at the beginning of a word? How many letters make the sound /r/? Write a spelling rule for each sound.

RULES

1. Say the sound /l/ when a word begins with the consonant letter _____ .
2. Say the sound /r/ when a word begins with the consonant letter _____ or the letters _____ _____ .

Here are some words with the sounds /l/ and /r/ at the end. Study the spelling of these words.

/l/	/r/
bowl	wear
meal	for
call	clear
spell	hair
sale	more
middle	picture

What letters make the sounds /l/ and /r/ at the end of a word? How many letters make the sounds /l/ and /r/? What about *e* at the end of a word? Write a spelling rule for each sound.

RULES

1. At the end of a word, you can find _______ or _______ consonant letter *l*'s for the sound /l/.
   The letter *e* at the end of a word is *(circle one)* pronounced not pronounced.
2. At the end of a word, you can find _______ consonant letter *r* for the sound /r/.
   The letter *e* at the end of a word is *(circle one)* pronounced not pronounced.

PARTNER 2

1b. LISTENING DISCRIMINATION AND SPEAKING. Pair Practice Words for /l/ and /r/.
PARTNER 2. Use this page. PARTNER 1. Turn to page 158.

DIRECTIONS: First you are the listener. Your partner will say some words. Circle the words you hear. Ask your partner to repeat any words you do not understand. Number 1 is an example.

1. (led) red
2. low row
3. lake rake
4. lip rip
5. load road
6. light right
7. long wrong
8. alive arrive

Now you are the speaker. Say the words to your partner. You see the consonant sound before each word. For example, you say "Number 9 is *lace*." Repeat any words your partner does not understand.

9. /l/ lace
10. /r/ correct
11. /l/ low
12. /r/ right
13. /l/ lock
14. /l/ led
15. /r/ wrong
16. /r/ rake

Now compare answers with your partner.

PARTNER 2

2b. LISTENING DISCRIMINATION AND SPEAKING. Pair Practice Sentences for /l/ and /r/.
PARTNER 2. Use this page. PARTNER 1. Turn to page 158.

DIRECTIONS: First you are the listener. Your partner will say some sentences. Circle the word you hear. Ask your partner to repeat any sentences you do not understand. Number 1 is an example.

1. This ______________ is heavy.
   a. lock b. (rock)
2. She has a ____________ number.
   a. long b. wrong
3. It's a picture of the ______________ .
   a. lace b. race
4. He sat by the ______________ .
   a. lake b. rake

Now you are the speaker. Say the sentences to your partner. You see the consonant sound before each sentence. Repeat any sentences your partner does not understand.

5. /l/ COLLECT the homework.
6. /r/ Do you have the RIGHT one?
7. /r/ I can't break this ROCK.
8. /l/ Put this on your LIST.

Now compare answers with your partner.

PARTNER 2

4b. SPEAKING AND LISTENING. Pair Practice for /l/ and /r/. PARTNER 2. Use this page. PARTNER 1. Turn to page 160.

DIRECTIONS: Here are results of an English test for different students. Your partner has some English test results, too. Take turns asking and answering questions. Make an X on the answers. Pronounce /l/ and /r/ correctly.

EXAMPLE:

YOU: How is Reza's grammar?
YOUR PARTNER: Excellent. How is Richard's reading?
YOU: Average. How is . . .

RESULTS OF ENGLISH TEST

Student	Skill	Test Results: Excellent	Very Good	Average	Below Average
Reza	Reading		X		
	Spelling			X	
	Grammar	✗			
	Pronunciation				
Helga	Reading				
	Spelling	X			
	Grammar				
	Pronunciation		X		
Richard	Reading			X	
	Spelling				
	Grammar				
	Pronunciation	X			
Rolfe	Reading				
	Spelling	X			
	Grammar		X		
	Pronunciation				
El-Ali	Reading			X	
	Spelling				
	Grammar	X			
	Pronunciation				
Lenore	Reading		X		
	Spelling			X	
	Grammar				
	Pronunciation				

Now compare answers with your partner.

PARTNER 2

5b. SPEAKING AND LISTENING. Where in the World? Pair Practice for /l/ and /r/.
PARTNER 2. Use this page. PARTNER 1. Turn to page 161.

DIRECTIONS: First your partner will ask you where some cities are. Answer with the country. Ask your partner to repeat any questions you do not understand. Your partner will tell you the answer if you do not know.

EXAMPLE:

YOUR PARTNER: Where in the world is Lima?
YOU: Lima is in Peru.

Now ask your partner where in the world the cities are. Repeat any questions your partner does not understand. If your partner does not know the answer, tell your partner the answer.

EXAMPLE:

YOU: Where in the world is Lima?
YOUR PARTNER: Lima is in Peru.

7. . . . Rome? (Italy)
8. . . . Teheran? (Iran)
9. . . . Seoul? (Korea)
10. . . . Beirut? (Lebanon)
11. . . . Paris? (France)
12. . . . Madrid? (Spain)

PARTNER 2

1b. LISTENING DISCRIMINATION AND SPEAKING. Pair Practice Words for /l/ and /r/ after Vowels. PARTNER 2. Use this page. PARTNER 1. Turn to page 164.

DIRECTIONS: First you are the listener. Your partner will say some words. Circle the words you hear. Ask your partner to repeat any words you do not understand. Number 1 is an example.

1.	all	(are)	5.	fail	fair
2.	ball	bar	6.	whale	wear
3.	feel	fear	7.	tail	tear
4.	wheel	we're	8.	towel	tower

Now you are the speaker. Say the words to your partner. You see the consonant sound after each word. For example, you say "Number 9 is *while*." Repeat any words your partner does not understand.

9.	while	/l/	13.	were	/r/
10.	pair	/r/	14.	car	/r/
11.	hear	/r/	15.	fail	/l/
12.	fall	/l/	16.	tail	/l/

Now compare answers with your partner.

PARTNER 2

2b. LISTENING DISCRIMINATION AND SPEAKING. Pair Practice Sentences for /l/ and /r/ after Vowels. PARTNER 2. Use this page. PARTNER 1. Turn to page 164.

DIRECTIONS: First you are the listener. Your partner will say some sentences. Circle the word you hear. Ask your partner to repeat any sentences you do not understand. Number 1 is an example.

1. He got a ________ yesterday.
   a. call b. (car)
2. Do you know the word "__________" ?
   a. while b. wire
3. We saw a __________ .
   a. towel b. tower
4. What do you __________ ?
   a. feel b. fear

Now you are the speaker. Say the sentences to your partner. You see the consonant sound before each sentence. Repeat any sentences your partner does not understand.

5. /r/ This coat has a TEAR.
6. /l/ She didn't say "ALL."
7. /r/ September is FAR.
8. /l/ You need a BALL to play the game.

Now compare answers with your partner.

PARTNER 2

4b. SPEAKING AND LISTENING. Pair Practice for /l/ and /r/ after Vowels. PARTNER 2. Use this page. PARTNER 1. Turn to page 166.

DIRECTIONS: You and your partner want to do some interesting things together next year. Here is your calendar. It shows some things you will do. Find out your partner's plans for next year. Take turns asking and answering questions. Pronounce /l/ and /r/ correctly.

EXAMPLE:

YOU: What are you going to do in November?
YOUR PARTNER: I'm going to volunteer at the library. What are you going to do in March?
YOU: I'm going to take a class to learn about computers. What are you . . .

MY CALENDAR

January: go to a classical ballet
February: take a trip to the state capital
March: take a class to learn about computers
April: work at a local laboratory
May: travel in Africa
June: write an article for a journal
July: take the children to Disneyland
August: tour a car factory
September: have jury duty at court
October: go to a professional conference in Baltimore
November: go to a lecture on solar energy
December: take a final exam in English

MY PARTNER'S CALENDAR

January ____________________
February ____________________
March ____________________
April ____________________
May ____________________
June ____________________
July ____________________
August ____________________
September ____________________
October ____________________
November ***Volunteer at the library***
December ____________________

What activities can you and your partner do together next year?